T0319162

Cambridge Elements ≡

Elements in the Economics of Emerging Markets
edited by
Bruno S. Sergi
Harvard University

ON THE ROAD TO ECONOMIC PROSPERITY

The Role of Infrastructure in Ghana

Tuan Anh Luong
De Montfort University

Zenas Azuma
De Montfort University

CAMBRIDGE
UNIVERSITY PRESS

Shaftesbury Road, Cambridge CB2 8EA, United Kingdom

One Liberty Plaza, 20th Floor, New York, NY 10006, USA

477 Williamstown Road, Port Melbourne, VIC 3207, Australia

314–321, 3rd Floor, Plot 3, Splendor Forum, Jasola District Centre, New Delhi – 110025, India

103 Penang Road, #05–06/07, Visioncrest Commercial, Singapore 238467

Cambridge University Press is part of Cambridge University Press & Assessment, a department of the University of Cambridge.

We share the University's mission to contribute to society through the pursuit of education, learning and research at the highest international levels of excellence.

www.cambridge.org
Information on this title: www.cambridge.org/9781009014397

DOI: 10.1017/9781009029360

© Tuan Anh Luong and Zenas Azuma 2022

First published 2022

A catalogue record for this publication is available from the British Library.

ISBN 978-1-009-01439-7 Paperback
ISSN 2631-8598 (online)
ISSN 2631-858X (print)

On the Road to Economic Prosperity

The Role of Infrastructure in Ghana

Elements in the Economics of Emerging Markets

DOI: 10.1017/9781009029360
First published online: October 2022

Tuan Anh Luong
De Montfort University

Zenas Azuma
De Montfort University

Author for correspondence: Tuan Anh Luong, Tuan.luong@dmu.ac.uk

Abstract: This Element investigates how the Ghanaian household wealth index is impacted by travel time reduction, which is a direct effect of infrastructural investments from 2000 to 2016. The wealth index is constructed based on the possession of selected assets and reflects the well-being of residents in Ghana. The Element employs two datasets, the Demographic and Health Survey (DHS) and the DHS covariates. The two-stage least square estimation is implemented to establish the causal relationship. The Element finds that a 10 percent reduction in travel time from 2000 to 2015 would result in a 1.2 percent increase in the wealth index from 2003 to 2016. This finding is robust to various settings, including the addition of more control variables, the use of different instrumental variables, and the study of both short-term and long-term effects. The analysis lends support to the Ghanaian government's current economic and infrastructure development plans.

Keywords: infrastructure, development economics, Ghana, emerging markets, road networks

ISBNs: 9781009014397 (PB), 9781009029360 (OC)
ISSNs: 2631-8598 (online), 2631-858X (print)

Contents

1 Executive Summary

Economic development requires a full-scale, high-quality infrastructure system. This is particularly true with transport infrastructure. Roads and railways are needed to allow an efficient commute to work and other social activities. They also connect markets at the local and global levels, enabling firms to provide goods and services at a large scale and thereby enhancing their profitability. Therefore, infrastructure can have transformative impacts on households and businesses.

It is estimated that by 2040, the gap between infrastructural needs (both transport and nontransport) and actual investment would be $15 trillion. Transports are the main sectors that require major investments. They account for more than half of global investment needs but the amount of resources invested has been inadequate. In the three sectors – roads, ports, and airports – the current investments are 30 percent below what is needed.[1]

There is no place where the problem is more pertinent than in Africa. Arguably the continent with the largest potential for growth, it only accounts for 6 percent of global infrastructure investment, far behind other continents such as Asia with more than half of the global share. Current estimates show that investment in infrastructure sectors only meets 57 percent of the demand for infrastructure in the continent, compared to 81 percent globally. The picture is similar when we focus on transport infrastructure. In all sectors from roads to rails and ports, the current investments only meet half of what is needed for economic growth. In many parts of the continent, people still lack access to basic utilities and are disconnected from the global market. This is adversely affecting their quality of life and hindering development in the region.

The current pandemic further highlights these needs. Countries that have good infrastructure systems were better prepared. High infection rates put a lot of strain on the healthcare systems, and social distancing meant that the transport system had to reduce its capacity. As a result, only the countries with extensive and resilient systems could ensure that basic services still function. Moreover, with countries planning economic programs to recover from the disastrous effects of the pandemic, the need for infrastructure investment is greater than ever.

In this Element, we assess the impacts of investment in transport infrastructure, with Ghana as our case study. Located in West Africa, Ghana is divided both geographically and economically by Lake Volta. Economic activities are concentrated in the southwest while the vast productive agricultural lands in the northeast are still waiting to be developed.

---

[1] Global Infrastructure Outlook. https://outlook.gihub.org/.

The country is in dire need of infrastructure investment in general, and transport infrastructure in particular. Rapid economic development in the country – with an annual output growth of 7 percent between 2017 and 2019 – calls for more infrastructure development, especially in the area of transport. Moreover, the quality of its infrastructure system is far below that of the best-performing countries in Africa. This is partly due to political instability with successive coups in the 1970s and 1980s following Ghana's independence in 1957.

Since the 1980s, the government of Ghana has put infrastructure investment as one of the key pillars of its development plan. The Road Fund was established in 1985 and restructured in 1997 to enhance road quality. Investments in the transport sectors took off, especially in the period from 2000 to 2016. The Road Fund's annual inflow was only 25.5 million Ghana cedi (or $3.89 million) in 2000 and surged to 272.6 million Ghana cedi in 2015. Even if we take into account inflation, this represents a 20 percent rise per year. In 2018, the Ghanaian government approved the Long-Term National Development Plan (LTNDP), an integral part of which was the

National Infrastructure Plan (NIP). The LTNDP is an ambitious plan that provides a visionary development picture for Ghana in the next forty years. This plan calls for a more quantitative investigation of how each of its components, such as the NIP, would contribute to the economic development of the country; such investigation is one of the main objectives of this Element.

Assessing the impacts of infrastructure investment has always been a challenging task for researchers. The measurement of infrastructure and the establishment of causation relationships are just some notable examples of such challenges. We solved these problems by using travel time reduction as a direct consequence of the investment in roads in Ghana in the first decade of the twenty-first century. We provided a theoretical framework that shows how time can be a component of wealth and, hence, a reduction in travel time, which would increase the time available for other activities, contributes to the rise in household wealth. This framework served as a guide in our empirical analysis.

We then applied the instrumental variable approach to establish causality. The instruments we employed are the length of the growing season and the slope of the terrain. They proved to be strong instruments that helped us uncover the effectiveness of infrastructure development in the country from 2000 to 2016.

To conduct our analysis, we made use of the Demographic and Health Survey (DHS) Program, which was set up by the United States Agency for International Development (USAID). Not only did it report the wealth index of Ghanaian households, which is our main economic outcome, but it also provided demographic information of these households. All of this information helped us control for confounding factors that might affect household wealth. Another database used in our research was the Demographic and Health Survey (DHS) Covariate Dataset, which reported the travel time to a metropolitan area from the clusters that the households lived in. Moreover, the information from this dataset helped us to construct the instrument variables that were crucial in our analysis.

Our analysis suggests that investment in infrastructural projects contributes to households' wealth via the reduction of travel time. Indeed, if households can commute to a metropolitan area 10 percent faster, their wealth would increase by 1.2 percent. This striking result has several important policy implications. First, it lends evidence-based support to the many infrastructural projects under the NIP that the government of Ghana has implemented since 2018. Second, it calls for more investment to fill the infrastructure gaps that we have observed in many parts of the world, especially in Africa. Third, it suggests that we need to make infrastructure investment inclusive because remote areas, from which commuting time to more developed areas has enormous potential to be reduced, are often underrepresented in the NIP plans. These implications lead to our final suggestion, namely to establish a high-quality and transparent institution for allocating investment fairly and efficiently. This will ensure investments are not politically motivated but aim to enhance efficiency. Moreover, such an institution will improve the effectiveness of the monitoring and assessment of investments.

2 Introduction

For the past two years, the COVID-19 pandemic has brought challenges to all aspects of life. Economically, it left a large scar that might takes years to heal. In half of the world, GDP in 2022 is still below the pre-pandemic level. Even in 2023, the number of these countries is predicted to remain high [1]. Economic development is, therefore, more important than ever to help bring life back to normal.

However, many challenges to economic development still lie ahead. One of them is the infrastructure investment gap. According to the latest reports, the gaps are large in all parts of the world. Take the United States as an example. Despite being the largest economy in the world, it still has a large gap to cover. The World Bank estimates that the US infrastructure gap from 2017 to 2040 is nearly $4 trillion, while the Infrastructure Investment and Jobs Act, signed in November 2021, only provided $1.2 trillion. The Next Generation EU, which is the European recovery plan, also fell short of the infrastructure needs of the continent [1]. The need to fill this gap has been a continuous one [2].

The frequency and ease of movement of factors of production that foster economic development have been acknowledged by many to be essential in causing the wheel of an economy to turn. The factors of production (land, labor, and capital) are fundamental to a thriving economy; however, in stagnation, these factors cannot attain their optimum economic productivity. In the wake of the COVID-19 pandemic, global economic productivity saw record lows due to restrictions in many western countries ([3], [4]). The hardship that came with these restrictions highlighted the importance of factor mobility to an economy.

The crucial role of factor mobility in economic development motivates us to investigate, in this Element, the impact of infrastructure on economic development. More precisely, our research question is whether the road system in Ghana, which was developed in the first decade of the twenty-first century and helped bring its residents closer to the metropolitan areas, was welfare enhancing.

Empirical research into the role of infrastructure in explaining economic development remains of paramount importance. The Global Infrastructure Outlook [5] reports Africa and Asia to be home to $6.3 trillion out of the $15 trillion global infrastructure gap. It is important to note that Africa is mainly inhabited by developing nations. In the case of Ghana, transport infrastructure is severely lacking in comparison to developed countries and certain emerging market economies. According to the CIA World Factbook [6], infrastructure in the country occupies the middle rank globally. For instance, roadways are ranked 45th, and waterways are ranked 56th. Some other means of transport are near the bottom with railways ranked 93rd and airports 154th.

Roadways are the primary means of transportation in Ghana. However, out of a total of 109,515 kilometers of road networks, only 13,787 kilometers were paved as of 2009 [6]. Traffic congestion, muddy roads, and flooding when it rained were significant factors that impaired mobility [7]. The quality of transport infrastructure is reflected in the safety and amount of time it takes to travel to specific destinations. In as much as good transport infrastructure can reduce travel time, poor transport infrastructure can increase travel time and hence reduce the rate of economic activity within a region.

The relevance of infrastructure in contributing to the development of a country has been explored extensively in the literature, especially after the seminal work by Aschauer, who, by setting an aggregate production technology in which public capital is one of the factors of production, derived a regression equation where labor productivity is a function of the ratio of public to private capital [8]. With this framework, he discovered that the presence of core infrastructure (e.g. roads, railways, water, etc.) was a strong predictor of productivity improvement. Following Aschauer, literature to prove infrastructure investment is essential in generating and sustaining long-term economic growth and competitiveness has been growing ([9], [10], [11], [12], [13]).

However, there is no consensus on the precise contribution it makes and the extent of its significance to economic growth ([14], [15]).

Ghana provides an ideal setting to investigate the role of infrastructure in economic development. Relative to other low-income countries, Ghana has a fairly modern infrastructure system. However, this system only contributed modestly to economic growth in the country. In the 2000s, only 1 percentage point of income per capita growth could be attributed to infrastructure. As a result, infrastructure has a huge potential that is still untapped. Raising the quality to that of other middle-income countries could boost Ghana's economic growth by nearly three percentage points [16].

To measure economic development, we depart from the literature where productivity, GDP, income per capita, and poverty alleviation have been used ([17], [18], [19]). Instead, we employ the wealth index, which is a composite measure of a household's cumulative living standard. This measure allows us to take a micro perspective. Indeed, the richness of our dataset allows us to exploit regional variation in infrastructure in Ghana. This variation is reflected in the heterogeneous changes in the reduction in travel time from where the households are located to a metropolitan area which will be defined more specifically later in this Element. Intuitively, shortened travel time accelerates productivity, which in turn accelerates the circular flow of economic activity and ultimately leads to increases in revenue, income, wealth, and an overall increase in economic development. A challenge to unraveling the role of infrastructure in the development of a country is establishing the causal relationship [20]. A solution to this problem is the instrumental variable approach [21]. Our main instrument is the length of the growing season. Our first-stage statistics show that it is a strong instrument. We find that a 10 percent reduction in the travel time to a metropolitan area would enhance the welfare index by 1.2 percent. To ensure our findings are robust, we carry out a battery of checks. More precisely, we include additional controls such as the regional wealth index or all the regional specific factors. We find that our results remain unchanged with respect to these specifications. We then test our results with alternative instruments and then with alternative dependent variables. The consistency of our results shows that infrastructure, and in particular the development of road networks in Ghana, did contribute in great part to enhancing the welfare of the households in the country.

What follows is an investigation of how infrastructure investment in Ghana in the first decade of the twenty-first century contributed to its economic development. In Section 3, we present the geographical landscape of the country and explain the need for infrastructure. We also provide an account of the historical, current, and future investment in infrastructure in the country.

Section 4 presents a review of related studies. We review how the concepts of economic development and infrastructure were discussed in the literature and provide the justification for our measurements. We review studies that investigate the impacts of infrastructure in general, and road development in particular, on economic development, especially in African countries. We also review papers that analyzed the relationship between time and household welfare. These papers help us build the theoretical and empirical framework for our analysis.

Section 5 introduces our research data. The first dataset is the DHS dataset, which was collected by the USAID. This dataset gives us the main economic outcome, which is the household wealth index; this is a composite index based on the possession of selected assets. At the same time, it reports household characteristics which are useful in controlling for confounding factors. The second dataset is the DHS covariate dataset, which includes the reduction in travel time to a metropolitan area, our main regressor. It also contains other information, such as the length of the growing season and the slope of the terrain. All of this information is important for constructing the instrumental variables.

In the first part of Section 6, we present a theoretical framework that shows how time can be considered as a component of household wealth. In particular, we show that time can have a price, as does any other tangible asset such as houses. With this framework, it becomes clear how investment in infrastructure that helps reduce travel time can increase household wealth. Indeed, this theoretical framework leads to the empirical settings used in our research. We then discuss the challenges associated with our approach and how to address these issues.

Section 7 presents the main results of our research. We first report the results with the conventional OLS approach. This approach, however, struggles to establish the causal relationship between our main regressor (travel time reduction) and the economic outcome (changes in wealth index). We then turn to the instrumental variable (IV) approach. We present first the tests of our IV to ensure the instruments we used are relevant and strong. We then present the estimates with this IV approach.

Section 8 checks if our results are robust to the different empirical settings. We first check if our results are robust to the addition of control variables. We use an alternative instrument variable, and then long-term instead of short-term economic outcomes as further robustness checks. Our tests confirm the consistency of our results across different settings.

Section 9 provides the policy implications of our analysis. It calls for continuous support for current development plans such as the NIP to fill the infrastructure investment gap, especially in remote areas which are often overlooked in the NIP plan. Such policies require a strong and transparent institutional system to ensure the resources of these plans are not diverted away. We then provide concluding remarks with suggestions for future research.

3 Background

3.1 The Geographical Landscape in Ghana

Ghana has a total aerial coverage of 238,533 square kilometers of which 227,533 square kilometers are land and 11,000 square kilometers are water. The landscape in Ghana is divided by Lake Volta (see Figure 1). South of the Lake are large, dense cities. Most of the resources in the country are concentrated in this region, which explains its low poverty rates. The North, however, is markedly different. Although this region, being relatively flat, is endowed with vast productive lands, these lands are mostly underused as the majority of the agricultural activities occur in the center of the country while services and manufacturing take place in the South. The particular landscape in Ghana dictates the distribution of the infrastructure system. With most of the economic activities concentrated in the South, it is not surprising that the infrastructure network is denser in this region. Ghana is home to ten airports (seven paved and three unpaved). Ghana's annual air traffic passengers numbered 467,438 in 2018 [6] and ranked 104th in the world [22]. The quality of airport infrastructure was ranked 112th in 2019 [22]. Ghana's railways span 947 kilometers; their quality was ranked 94th globally [22]. Roadways in Ghana have an aerial span of 109,515 kilometers (13,787 paved and 95,728 unpaved) with a quality rank of 117th [22]. Ghana's waterways cover a span of 1,293 kilometers, which includes 168 kilometers for lighters and launches in the Tano River, Ankobra River, and Volta Lake, and 1,125 kilometers of the feeder and arterial waterways. The quality rank of port infrastructure was 111th [22]. The port traffic rank was 63rd. Ghana also has two major seaports in Tema and Takoradi [6].

3.1.1 Air Transport

In an attempt to expand its transport infrastructure, the Ghanaian government embarked on a variety of transport infrastructure projects. Air travel infrastructure improvement included the refurbishing of Terminal 2 of the Kotoka International Airport, with an improved arrival hall (with new immigration booths), newly installed baggage carousels, and newly installed eGates. The Kumasi International Airport saw the construction of a modernized runway and

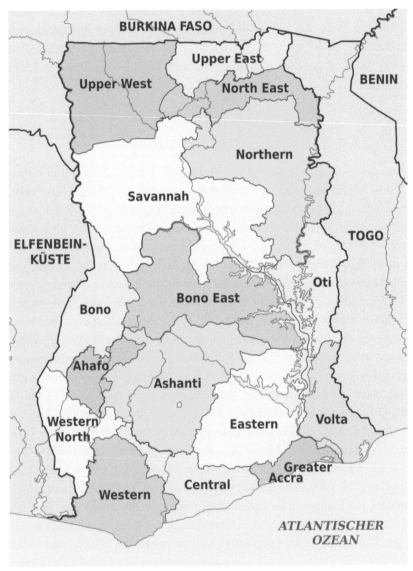

Figure 1 The map of Ghana

Source: Wikipedia.

the installation of instrument landing systems with aeronautical ground light-ning. Furthermore, there are plans to construct an ultramodern terminal and a runway extension to make room for medium-sized aircraft. New projects also include the construction of the Ho airport. Additionally, the government is working on constructing a new state-of-the-art export, import, and transit cargo center in Accra, the country's capital city.

3.1.2 Maritime Transport

The government plans to expand its maritime infrastructure to accommodate rising pressure from landlocked neighboring countries and the business community. An investment of $1.5 billion has been put into the Tema ports expansion, adding four 1,400-meter-long berths, with a container traffic capacity of 3 million twenty-foot equivalent units (TEUs). The government finished a 1.15-kilometer extension and construction of a leeside breakwater on the Takoradi port and has embarked on the second phase of that project to create more berthing facilities for bauxite, manganese, clinker, and limestone. Furthermore, to accommodate more refrigerated containers, an 800 TEU Reefer terminal has been constructed on the Takoradi port. Moreover, to monitor Ghana's exclusive economic zone and coastline, the Ghana Maritime Authority installed a vessel traffic management information system (which is a twenty-four-hour electronic surveillance system). Improvements are being made to the Takoradi logistic platform to provide warehousing facilities for the oil and gas industries. A $700-million port is also being constructed with a logistic supply base, a fabrication yard, a rig, and ship repair facilities that will create about 1,000 jobs.

3.1.3 Railways

The government has recently devised the Ghana Railway Master Plan which entails the modernization and reconstruction of existing rail networks (see Figure 2). The plan will initially focus on the southern part of the country before extending to the country's northern parts. Following this plan, the government has seen the completion of the Sekondi-Takoradi via Kojokrom rail line with the deployment of multiple train units on the line [7]. The front-end engineering design (FEED) for the Takoradi to Kumasi rail line with a connecting line from Dankwa to Awaso (Western Railway line) has also been completed. Furthermore, ongoing is the construction of a new train station in Sekondi, as well as extra construction work at the Butuah and Takoradi train stations. Ongoing FEED work at the time of this publication included the Accra to Nsawam line and the Eastern Railway line from Tema via Accra to Kumasi ([23], [24]. A recent project, named the Trans-Ecowas Railway, was jointly proposed by the governments of Ghana, Togo, and Côte d'Ivoire. This 550-kilometer railway line will cost $3.8 billion and run from Elubo at the Côte d'Ivoire border to Aflao at the Togo border with a line that branches to Keta. This is in line with the United Nations' Sustainable Development Goals and the African Union Agenda 2063. However, in recent years, Ghana has abandoned some of its infrastructural projects such as the 194-kilometer skytrain due to high costs [25].

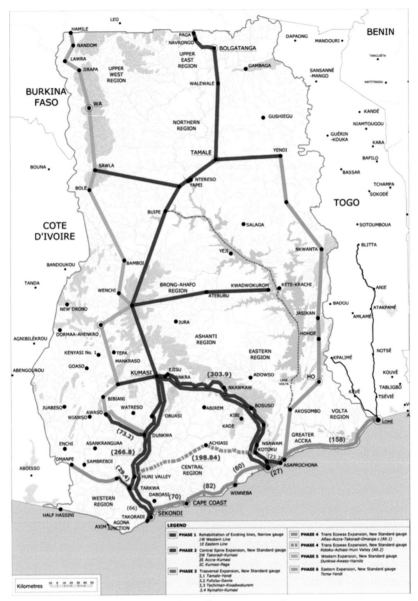

Figure 2 The railway master plan.
Source: Ministry of Railways Development, Ghana.

3.1.4 Road Networks

As far as the road network is concerned, the achievements have been relatively remarkable. The road sector grew at an annual rate of 8 percent [26]. Three main national road corridors (N2, N10, and N12) were constructed to connect the

North and the South. Another three national routes link the East and the West of the country (see Figure 3). The road connectivity is geared toward enhancing more networks between the northern and southern parts of Ghana, and currently, there are very few roads connecting the western and eastern parts. This is particularly true in the South, as the road network from the southwest to the

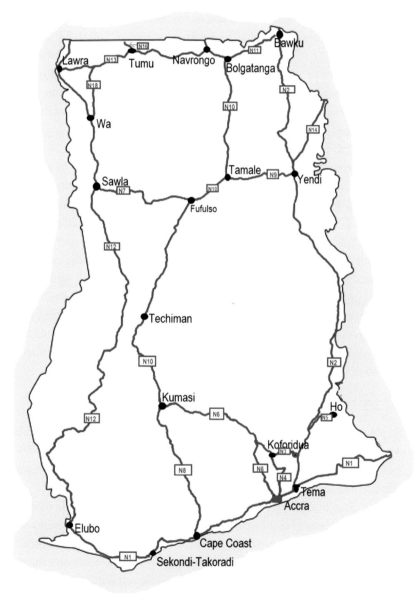

Figure 3 The national highway network in Ghana.
Source: Wikipedia

southeast is especially sparse. The distances households in the western and eastern regions need to travel to reach the major highway networks appear to be much longer compared to those for households in other regions. As a result, travel time is longer and market accessibility is more difficult in the western and eastern regions. In the west, however, the Bono region is the most connected. It is served by two national highway networks, the N10 and N12 highways.

In general, Ghana's road network is close to what is expected of a middle-income country. Total national road coverage went up from 67,450 kilometers in 2010 to 71,063 kilometers in 2014 [27]. The road densities are 158 and 804 kilometers per 1,000 square meters for paved and unpaved roads, respectively. Three-quarters of the roads are in fair or good condition. As a result, the average annual daily traffic is 1,300 cars per day on paved roads and 40 on unpaved roads [16].

The road network is the main form of transportation for Ghanaians. A report by the government suggested that road transportation accounts for more than 90 percent of traffic in the country [28]. The heavy reliance on this type of transportation has led to many problems, from traffic congestion to road degradation [29]. Due to the territorial landscape, only a quarter of the population has access to all-season roads within a two-kilometer radius. Raising this ratio to the standard in other African middle-income countries would require substantial investment. Moreover, about one-third of the road network is under intensive use (i.e. by more than 300 vehicles per day). This prompts concern about the sustainability of the road network. Other challenges to investment in road infrastructure are related to the financial situation of the government, namely the capacity to raise investments and revenue mobilization [30].

3.2 The Need for Infrastructure Investments in Ghana

A 2015 publication by the Ghanaian government highlights Ghana's motorable road network as of paramount importance [7]. Indeed, it is deemed a prerequisite to opening up the economy, reducing congestion, boosting economic activity, and decreasing road accidents.

Ghana's infrastructure indicators, relative to other African middle-income countries, remain low [31]. In terms of infrastructure quality, Ghana ranks far below the best-performing countries in Africa [22]. In addition, it is reported that while Ghana is doing well economically, its growth is not sustainable due to the serious gap between needs and available economic and social infrastructure [31]. Indeed, there is a growing demand for infrastructure in Ghana given the expanding population and the increasing pressure on the existing infrastructure.

In addressing these challenges, the Government of Ghana (GoG) has identified the need to partner with the private sector to fill the gaps in infrastructure. It is estimated that Ghana requires $1.5 billion per annum over the next few years to bridge the deficit in infrastructure [32]. The country's spending on infrastructure is about $1.2 billion per year, equivalent to 7.5 percent of the nation's GDP [33]. That leaves a gap of $300 million to be filled annually.

Despite multiple government plans to make substantial investments in road transport infrastructure, some projects have reverted to deplorable states after construction. One such project is the $166 million Fufulso-Sawla road. Financed with a loan from the African Development Bank in 2010, the road project was meant to foster regional integration between Ghana and countries situated at its northern border to improve international traffic. However, six years after the road's completion and opening, the road is currently in a dilapidated condition. This raises important questions regarding the longevity of the transport infrastructure projects being undertaken in Ghana, the actual level of connectivity, and transport costs.

3.3 History of Infrastructure Development in Ghana

The history of infrastructure development in Ghana started in the late nineteenth century when the British colonized the country and built the first railroads in the western region in 1898. The aims were to preserve their military control and to foster regional trade that had been restrained by prohibitive transportation costs. Further railroad lines were added in the eastern region at the beginning of the twentieth century. The country gained independence in 1957 and took charge of developing its infrastructure, investing heavily in many sectors such as energy, and railway and road transportation. A notable example was the construction of a hydroelectric dam on the Volta River, called the Akosombo Dam, to provide electricity for the aluminum industry. At the time, this construction was the largest investment in the Ghanaian government's economic development plan. The momentum was halted by the 1966 military coup that truncated all development plans. Subsequent projects were abandoned. Most of the policies to revive the infrastructure were either short-term or without any clear plan. Successive coups in the 1970s and 1980s continued to hold back the country's development. Economic growth was lacking, and debts and inflation were soaring. As a result, the government projects lacked funding [34]. It was not until 1983 that the government started to revive its economy with the Economic Recovery Program. Guided by the World Bank and the International Monetary Fund, the program aimed to restructure the economy and help the country gradually recover.

3.4 Infrastructure Investment from 2000 to 2016

In 1985, the government of Ghana set up the Road Fund with the main objective of creating more funding channels for road maintenance. In 1997, Act 536 was passed to restructure the Road Fund. This Act is therefore also called the Road Fund Act. The Act expanded the Road Fund mandate to other activities such as the upgrading and rehabilitation of roads and road safety activities. The Fund is managed by a management board comprising representatives from both government agencies and relevant interest groups. Management board members from the government have included representatives from the Ministry of Roads and Transport, representatives from the Ministry of Finance, the minister for mines and energy, the accountant general, the minister for local government and rural development, and two persons nominated outside the Ministry of Roads and Transport. Management board members from interest groups included representatives from the Association of Road Contractors, the Ghana Private Road Transport Union (GPRTU), the Ghana Private Enterprise Foundation, the Ghana Road Haulage Association, the Ghana Institute of Engineers, and the Ghana Association of Farmers and Fishermen. The Road Fund received praise that it followed and met nearly all the best practice guidelines [16]. It levied a fuel tax to maintain its road network. Substantial resources were poured into the road sectors. The average spending was around 1.5 percent of GDP and was distributed equally between the urban and rural areas.

Since the Fund was established and restructured, investment in road development in Ghana took off. In 2002, the inflow of revenue was only 31.2 million Ghana cedi (or $4.76 million). It rose to 108.6 million Ghana cedi in 2006, an annual growth rate of 60 percent. Another surge took place between 2011 and 2015 with an annual growth rate of 40 percent [35].

During the same period, Ghana's economy has been successfully growing. It has a diverse structure where agriculture, manufacturing, and services accounted for 18.3, 24.5, and 57.2 percent of GDP in 2017 [36]. The country is a very active trade partner not only in the region but also globally. In 2021, its trade balance exceeded $28 billion.[2] As a result of economic growth, poverty levels have dropped significantly. Ghana reduced its incidence of multidimensional poverty by nine percentage points from 55 percent in 2011 to 46 percent in 2017 [37].

3.5 The Long-Term National Development Plan

In 2018, the GoG started a Long-term National Development Plan (LNDP) to address major problems that remained after the completion of five medium-term plans from 1996 to 2017. One of these problems was inadequate infrastructure

---

[2] www.bog.gov.gh/economic-data/merchandise-trade-flows/

that prevented efficient service delivery and pegged back the country [38]. Having realized the lack of a coherent vision that could have linked the previous plans, the GoG decided to create a vision for their development over the next forty years, from 2018 to 2057. It consists of ten medium-term plans, each of which corresponds to an election cycle. These medium-term plans are then translated into annual plans and budgets. The LNDP contains six integral components:

(1) National Infrastructure Plan
(2) National Human Capital Development Strategy
(3) Economic Growth Strategy
(4) Spatial Development Framework
(5) Sustainable Development Goals, Agenda 2063 and other Global Development Frameworks
(6) Social, Economic, Environmental and Institutional Policies and Strategies.

All of these strategies are to realize the long-term goals set by the LNDP, which are to (1) build an industrialized, inclusive, and resilient economy; (2) create an equitable, healthy, and disciplined society; (3) build safe, well-planned, and sustainable communities; (4) build effective, efficient, and dynamic institutions, and (5) strengthen Ghana's role in international affairs. The next section will discuss the National Infrastructure Plan specifically.

3.6 The National Infrastructure Plan

The purpose of the National Infrastructure Plan (NIP) is to harmonize the development of infrastructure projects in the country. The vision of the National Development Planning Commission (NDPC), which coordinates the NIP, is to establish high-quality infrastructure assets that are efficient, reliable, resilient, and inclusive. Such a system is crucial for supporting the export-led growth strategy and for enhancing the welfare of Ghanaians.

The NIP consists of seven categories including energy, transport, human settlements, water, information and communication technology, institution developments, and logistics. They are all implemented in an integrated manner to ensure a coordinated provision of critical infrastructure services. Out of the various categories, transportation is the most important with ten projects in the pipeline. These projects are presented in Table 1.

4 Literature Review

4.1 The Concept of Economic Development and Wealth

According to the *Oxford Dictionary of Economics* [39], economic development is the economic transformation of a country or region that leads to improvement

Table 1 The National Infrastructure Plan

Projects	Description
Metro/light rail transit system	The project is located in Kumasi, the second-largest city in Ghana. It is expected to kick-start in 2025 and will strengthen the city's transport system by alleviating the urban mobility deficiency that has inhibited the city's economic growth.
Central spine rail line	A rail line system from the central district of Kumasi to other major cities such as Mankranso, Bechem, Sunyani, Techiman, Kintampo, Buipe, Tamale, Walewale, Bolgatanga, and Navrongo. The rail line ends at Paga, a city on the Burkina Faso border. The project will start in 2023 and aims to connect Ghana and Burkina Faso to open up further economic opportunities.
Trans-ECOWAS Railway Line	The estimated 550 kilometers of railways will connect the southwest and southeast regions of the country, ensuring a smooth and rapid movement of people and goods not only within the nation but also with neighboring countries including Togo, Cote d'Ivoire, Benin, Nigeria, Liberia, and Sierra Leone.
Establishment of home-based carrier	The project is located in Accra and aims to make Kotoka International Airport an aviation hub. It will promote tourism, trade, and investment in Ghana and West Africa.

Project	Description
Volta Lake Transport System	The project will connect the eastern multimodal transport corridor to the railways from Tema to Mpakadan. The aim is to upgrade the capacity of cargo transport along Lake Volta.
Airport City II	A commercial hub in Accra with hotels, shopping malls, parks, residential facilities, and intermodal transport terminals.
Tamale Airport MRO Facility	The project will provide more facilities, including maintenance, repair, and overhaul (MRO), to Tamale Airport to connect Ghana and the West Africa sub-region.
Air Cargo Facility	The project will develop the air cargo facility at Tamale Airport to foster the trading activities with the West Africa sub-region.
Green Airports (G-Gap)	A partnership with private sectors to provide solar panels in airports in Ghana, to meet their increasing demand for energy.
Keta Sea Port	A third port in the country will be built in Keta, which will ease the strains on the two existing ports.

of the well-being and economic capabilities of its residents. Distinctively, while economic growth observes the quantified changes within a given economy through observing the per capita or regional (national) income, economic development reflects the changes in investment, income, and savings accompanied by incremental technological and institutional changes in a nation's social and economic structure.

In his seminal work, [40] emphasizes that the accelerated income and prices within a given economy generate cumulative expansion as they lead to incremental purchasing power, which translates into increased demand and subsequently increased supply. This concept of accelerated income and its link to economic development remains fundamental to the concept of the circular flow of economic activity model. The circular flow theory highlights the relevance of household income to economic development. However, the concept of income can be taken further through its association with wealth. Income refers to the regular stream of money acquired through work or investment. Wealth, on the other hand, can be defined as the total value of a person's net assets ([39], p.173). It has several advantages over income and consumption as a measure of the household economic welfare. It is stable and less subjective to measurement errors because the assets to compute wealth are observable. Moreover, the process of calculating wealth is less costly in terms of time and money because these assets are often readily available. As a result, this process can be applied to a wide range of households which enhances the quality of the analyzes. Wealth can also be explained as valuable economic assets in the form of either physical goods or monetary value accumulated over time. Accumulated income and valuable possession over time translate into wealth. Without income, wealth cannot be maintained as the cost of living depletes assets and financial reserves. Considering this, household wealth will be employed as an indicator of social-economic development.

4.2 The Measures of Infrastructure

There are essentially two ways to define infrastructure. The first way is to establish a concept of infrastructure. The notion of infrastructure was first mentioned in the early theories of economic development. According to these theories, infrastructure was needed as a big push to overcome the vicious cycle in which low productivity led to low income, low savings, and low investment [41]. They prompted the calls for Keynesian macroeconomic policies where more attention should be paid to basic industries such as roads or power [42]. Another idea was proposed by [43] where he considered infrastructure sectors as other productive sectors. He then called for the central planners' balancing of all sectors.

The switch from early development theories came in the 1950s when the World Bank viewed infrastructure as social overhead capital [44]. According to their definition, infrastructure was capital shared by many (social) but not attributable to any productive activity (overhead). [45], one of the leading economists in the World Bank, went further, regarding infrastructure as capital that provides public services and that should be the priority of the World Bank's programs.

The concept of infrastructure as we know it today started to take shape in the 1960s. It became omnipresent in popular journalism and official documents. For instance, it started to appear in the country analyzes issued by the World Bank. It has been deemed a prerequisite for economic development, especially in developing countries. This approach is, however, abstract and therefore of little use in academic research. Subsequent research then viewed infrastructure as public expenditure or public investment ([46], [47], [48], [49], [50], [51], [52], [53], [54], [55], [56], [57]). There are several problems with this approach. For example, public expenditure is a more general concept than infrastructure as it also covers military and pension expenditure, among others. Moreover, it is hard to distinguish the quantity and quality of infrastructure within public expenditure.

A second way of looking at infrastructure is by providing a list of possible infrastructure goods. One can label infrastructure as transport, energy, communication, water, etc. With this view, researchers can analyze the impacts of each type of infrastructure independently. [58] found that telecommunication development had a significant impact on economic growth in the OECD from 1970 to 1990. Similarly, [59] quantified the effect of broadband infrastructure on economic growth in the OECD countries from 1996 to 2007, and found that a 10-percentage point increase in broadband penetration raised annual per capita growth by 0.9–1.5 percentage points. Wastewater treatment and transport systems were shown to have significant importance in the economic growth of developing countries [60]. [17] found evidence that being close to the transportation networks in China resulted in higher income per capita across sectors.

The problem with this approach is that infrastructure has multiple facets. Omitting one or several of them, especially when they are relevant to growth, can lead to invalid inferences. However, if we consider simultaneously multiple sectors of infrastructure in an econometric model, the estimates are likely to be imprecise. A solution to this problem is to develop a composite index that combines different sectors of infrastructure. [61] applied several techniques, including principle component analysis [62], the unobserved components method [63], and the quartile aggregation index [12] to provide aggregate indices on four broad categories of infrastructure: telecommunications, energy, roads, and railways. [64] defined the synthetic infrastructure quantity and quality indices using the principal component method. Although these techniques reduce the number of infrastructural dimensions, and therefore consolidate the regression equations, they overlook several mechanisms through which infrastructure could affect economic growth, including the externality effect, economies of scale, and the competition effect.

Finally, one important issue with measuring infrastructure is whether to use the flows or the stocks of infrastructure. Early literature paid more attention to the former (i.e. the public expenditure or investment). Findings with this type of measure are inconclusive. Depending on the empirical strategy (i.e. whether some controls are included), the effects of infrastructure can range from positive to insignificant ([14], [65]). These mixed results can be explained by several issues related to this type of measure. Indeed, there is no clear distinction between public and private capital. Even public capital could be invested in noninfrastructural activities such as military and security services or pensions. There are also the issues of whether public investment results in the accumulation of infrastructure due to mismanagement and whether this accumulation translates into the provision of infrastructural services because of inefficiencies.

These problems prompted a growing recent literature that uses the physical stock of literature ([17], [61], [64], [66], [67], [68]). However, as in other types of capital, it is a challenging task to account for the different sectors of infrastructure when there are large differences. For instance, how do we add the length of roads that have been developed with the number of base stations in telecommunication? There are essentially two solutions to this problem. The first involves focusing on one infrastructure sector, such as roads ([69], [70]) or telecommunication [59]. The second is to develop a composite index that reflects the quantity and quality of all the relevant sectors in a parsimonious way, as we have discussed.

4.3 Infrastructure as a Prerequisite for Economic Development

Public capital had not been the subject of economic research until the 1970s. Conceptually, [71] considered infrastructure as a factor of production, similar to other factors such as labor and capital. Not only did infrastructure contribute directly to aggregate production, it also raised the productivity of complementary factors. This view was, however, challenged by [72], in whose endogenous growth model, the government chooses the level of public investments to maximize the economy's growth rate or welfare. If the rate of return of public investment is high enough, which reflects the important role of infrastructure, the government will divert the resources away from other activities toward infrastructure. In other words, there is a crowding-out effect. More investment in infrastructure crowds out the employment of other inputs.

It is important to note that infrastructure could take the form of stocks or flows. The former yields analytical tractability, as in [71] and [72]. However, the service of infrastructure, such as road transport, often takes the latter form. It takes time to build up the stock of infrastructure. As a result, the level of infrastructure that maximizes welfare is lower than [72] predicted [73]. If we consider both the flows and stocks of infrastructure, the levels of infrastructure to maximize growth and welfare are different. It requires more public investment to maximize growth than to maximize welfare ([74], [75]).

In addition to serving as a direct input in the aggregate production function, infrastructure can play a supporting factor to raise total factor productivity. Potentially, infrastructure generates the spillover externalities that benefit other inputs [76]. Transport and telecommunication reduce the costs of producing intermediate inputs and facilitate innovation ([77], [78]). Moreover, infrastructure helps accumulate other factors. Improved transport networks helped install new capitals [79] while more access to electricity enhanced educational attainment and reduced the cost of human capital accumulation [80].

Understanding theoretically how infrastructure contributed to economic development is one thing, but measuring the magnitude of the effect quantitatively is another matter. It was only in the late 1980s, when Aschauer presented a series of papers ([8], [81], [82]), that the empirical studies on this subject took off. Aschauer assumed a production technology where capital is distinctively separated into private and public (nonmilitary) capital. Productivity, defined as output per capita (or labor productivity), was then expressed as a function of labor, the capital utilization rate, and more importantly, the ratio of private and public investments to gross output. The signs of the coefficients of these ratios indicated the direction in which private and public investment contributed to the growth of labor productivity. More precisely, if these coefficients were positive (negative), capital investment would contribute positively (negatively) to the growth of labor productivity. With this idea, [8] demonstrated that most of the US decline in productivity in the 1970s was due to the drop in public investment. An important part of infrastructure was the core infrastructure such as transportation. It accounted for more than half of nonmilitary public capital stock. A 10 percent increase in investment in core infrastructure resulted in a 2.4 percent improvement in productivity. Aschauer then further strengthened his argument by explicitly categorizing public investment in consumption and investment. Using data from the G7 countries from 1966 to 1985, [82] showed that if the share of public consumption rose by 10 percent, labor productivity would decline by 1 percentage point. There was some concern that public investment might crowd out private investments [83], but it proved to be not a big issue in [81].

Following Aschauer's idea, other studies estimated the elasticities of national production with respect to infrastructure. An issue with [8]'s estimates was the aggregate time-series data that were subject to common trends. This problem led to spurious correlations and, hence, the estimates were implausibly large [84]. To address this issue, better techniques were used with various types of data, from subnational to national ones. For instance, applying the panel data technique with state-level data in the United States from 1969 to 1986, [65] suggested that the elasticity of public sector capital was not significantly different from 0. Using similar data but with the time series technique, [85] agreed with [65]. Moving to national accounts, [86] found that the average output elasticity of public capital was 0.1.

Most of the aforementioned studies employed the linear production function, including the Cobb-Douglas one. In these types of functions, total factor productivity (TFP) is a constant, which makes it harder to assess the impact of infrastructure on TFP. As a result, these types of models are not adequate ([51], [87]). More recent studies applied an alternative approach to allow more flexibility in studying the impact of infrastructure. [76] applied a growth-decomposition approach but failed to find any significant impact of public capital. However, the effect became significant when one allowed for nonlinear production [88]. [89] applied the dual cost function approach and found that the increase in infrastructure in Sweden from 1960 to 1988 reduced the private sector costs. [90] employed a similar technique to show that intrastate infra-structure in the United States from 1982 to 1996, via the spatial spillover, led to significant cost savings. Alternatively, public capital resulted in more output and higher profits [91].

Besides infrastructure in general, recent literature has also paid attention to infrastructural sectors that showed large effects. Using India's state-level data, [92] uncovered substantial externality effect from infrastructure to manufactur-ing productivity. They found that road development and enhanced electricity-generating capacity had contributed to more than half of TFP in India. Technological growth, which is proxied to TFP, could be boosted by informa-tion technology such as the Internet [93] and by electricity provision [94].

The effect of infrastructure investment is not limited to productivity but also extends to international trade, economic competitiveness, cost of supply, devel-opment, and growth ([10], [13]). They typically employed a reduced-form growth-regression framework relating long-run growth to suitable indicators of infrastructure, public capital, or public investment. The findings, especially for growth, are mixed. Employing historical data, [95] suggested that investment in transport and communication is consistently correlated with growth. Indeed, investment in infrastructure had a positive influence on growth via the economies of scale, the existence of network externalities and competition enhancing effects [96]. On the other side, [14] and [97] found no significant growth effects of infrastructure across US states and metropolitan areas. If we dig deeper into the data, we might find more clear-cut results. Indeed, different cross-country datasets for developing countries explained why [[98] found a negative relationship between the share of infrastructure in total public expenditure and economic growth, while [99] found the opposite result. In [100], the impacts of infrastructure varied by the infrastructural sectors. Moving beyond economic growth, [101] argued that well-established infrastructure promoted inclusivity and alleviated poverty, particularly in developing regions, and further showed that infrastructure was connected to economic development via the channels of economic growth, poverty alleviation, and a sustainable environment.

The evidence that infrastructure is conducive to economic development does have a fair number of critics. The first critic focused on the measure of infrastructure. Indeed, the most common measure is public investments or public spending on infrastructure. This aggregate measure tends to be nonstationary and drifts over time, as we have mentioned, which led to unrealistically large effects. Therefore, its trends should be subtracted from the original measure to avoid the spurious correlation problem ([102], [103]). [104] applied the first-differencing method to remove potential common trends. In addition to controlling for unobserved time-invariant fixed effects, this method deals with the nonstationarity of the time-series data [56]. More refined techniques were then subsequently adopted. For example, [105] used pooled mean group estimators, which unrestricted short-run parameter heterogeneity across countries while imposing (testable) restrictions on long-run parameter homogeneity.

First-differencing aggregate infrastructure investment is, however, not the ideal solution. With the first-differencing measures, the return on infrastructure became rather small [20]. Moreover, the estimated coefficients are often implausible because this method requires the impacts to be contemporary ([104], [106], [107]). In fact, it is unlikely that we can see the fruits of infrastructure development in the short term. As a result, the first-differencing method does not allow us to investigate any long-term relationship between infrastructure and economic development.

Another problem when using investments as a measure of infrastructure relates to their ownership. If we only focus on public investments, the results will be underestimated because private investments in infrastructure are significant. At its peak, private investment reached nearly $200 billion in developing countries alone [108]. It is, however, a challenging task to measure private investment. In many cases, data on private investments are not available. Even when it is available, the measures are dubious as it is not easy to distinguish infrastructure capital from other forms of capital [84]. Moreover, money can be diverted from its intended use. Indeed, in many developing countries, investments claimed to be used for infrastructure development could be wasted by corruption ([109], [110], [111]) or poor management ([112], [113]. These problems will undoubtedly lead to an underestimation of the impacts of infrastructure.

When establishing the causal relationship between infrastructure and economic development, especially when investment is used as a measure, a production function is often specified. The idea is to include public capital as an additional input besides labor and private capital in the production function. The share of public capital, which is to be estimated from the function, will indicate the rate of return on public capital and its contribution to labor productivity [8]. There are several criticisms to this approach. The first criticism is the measure of public capital, which we have discussed. One suggestion is to replace the aggregate public capital with the core infrastructure that includes highways and water systems [114] but the estimates are still implausible [84]. Even if all the variables are measured correctly, there is still an endogeneity issue as the quantity of labor hired by the firm might depend on its productivity, which is unobserved by the econometricians [115].

To avoid all of these problems, we depart from the literature by focusing on one type of infrastructure, roads. Instead of measuring investment in roads, we use the reduction of travel time – a direct impact of road development – and measure its impact on economic development. Indeed, our measure is not subject to the nonstationary problem. Moreover, we can measure the impact regardless of whether it results from public or private capital. In addition, we do not have to estimate a production function, which is still a challenging task for researchers [116]. In the next section, we will review the literature that investigates the impact of road development.

4.4 Impact of Road Developments

A direct effect of road development is to reduce transportation costs. Improvements in the road system result in higher travel speed, less congestion, and lower waiting or transfer time. This saved time then can be used to perform other activities, which enhance the welfare of road users. [117] employed this concept to measure the value of the time saved by these improvements and found that travel time savings were the largest component of benefits to road users.

As a result, saving travel time was often the main reason to develop urban transport projects [118]. In addition, road developments reduce the cost of traveling between cities and villages and enhance market access. [119] investigated the impact of the US Interstate Highway System, the construction of which was approved in 1956 and completed in 1978. The objectives of this system were to link metropolitan areas in the States. Although not intended, many rural counties were also connected to the Interstate Highways to enhance the national defense capabilities. [119] showed that the Interstate Highway System had greatly benefited rural counties via increases in their trading activities. Both the retail sector and the transportation sector, especially the trucking industry, saw a surge in revenues and income thanks to the reduction in trade barriers. Indeed, it was shown that driving activities in the United States increased with the development of these interstate highways, especially commercial driving and trucking [120]. New and improved highway networks also benefit the performance of firms. [121] assessed the impacts of a major road improvement program in India, the Golden Quadrilateral Program (GQP), and found that firms located on the highways targeted by the program significantly improved their inventory management and reduced their input costs by switching suppliers.

Interestingly, the impact of highway networks varies with the geographical scale. In [20], the smaller the scale, the smaller the impact, suggesting that a spillover effect could be in place. However, evidence of the spillover effect is mixed. Using data from seventeen regions in Spain between 1970 and 1995, [122] found that the aggregate effect of public capital could only be explained when the spillover effects were considered. [14] found no significant spillover effect in the forty-eight states in the United States between 1969 to 1986. Even negative effects were found in [123].

Road development can be extended to forms other than highways. [124] investigated the historical impact of railroads on the US economy. Like highways, railroads also resulted in greater market access for the connected counties. As a result, the rate of return on agricultural lands in these counties increased significantly. The researchers showed that removing all railroads in 1890 would have decreased the total value of agricultural lands in the United States by as much as 60 percent.

The impacts of road development are not limited to developed countries such as the United States but also occurred in developing countries. During the past decades, China invested heavily in its infrastructure. From 1978 to 2006, the annual growth rate of highways in China was 8.9 percent [125]. The large-scale transport infrastructure investments were to connect metropolitan centers in East China as well as the land-locked peripheral regions in Western China. [126] made use of China's National Trunk Highway System as a large-scale natural experiment. He found evidence of more trading activities between peripheral and metropolitan regions thanks to the falling trade costs. At the same time, GDP growth in counties that were not in this highway system fell significantly. Indeed, industrial output growth in these regions plummeted. In India, [127] showed that India's vast railroad network, which was built by the British government in the nineteenth century, reduced trade costs and, hence, the price gaps between regions in India. As a result, both interregional and international trade surged, which boosted the real income of Indian residents. In addition to the direct effects of reducing trade costs, road developments could have indirect effects on economic activities. [128] investigated the impacts of the GQP in India which led to an upgrade in the central highway network. Not only did it result in more manufacturing activities but the quality and efficiency of these activities also improved. Indeed, the allocative efficiency gain from this project was estimated to be 7.4 percent [129]. Using firm-level longitudinal data from Britain, [18] found that new transport infrastructure reorganized production activities and enhanced labor productivity, especially in establishments that benefit most from transport accessibility. [130] showed that the decentralization process followed road investments. In particular, while radial highways decentralized service sector activity, radial railroads decentralized industrial activity, and ring roads decentralized both.

Finally, new road infrastructure was shown to have impacts beyond increasing economic activities. It could alleviate income inequality, especially in developing countries [61]. It also results in human migration. Highways passing through cities would reduce their population by 18 percent [131]. Similarly, ring roads would move as much as 20 percent of the population in cities to surrounding areas [130].

4.5 Infrastructure in the Development of Africa

Africa is an ideal place to study the impacts of infrastructure on economic development. In many development indicators, from income per capita to life expectancy and human development indexes, African countries occupy most of the bottom places. Nearly half of Africa's population lives in landlocked countries. This geographic feature, together with substandard infrastructure performance, means that transport costs are extremely high and deprive its people of many opportunities in the global market [132]. The effects are not limited to trade barriers but extend to other aspects. The lack of infrastructure increased transaction costs and reduced market access to many agricultural and nonagricultural goods in Africa. [133] showed that improving the productivity in the transportation sector in Africa resulted in a significant rise in GDP in these countries. Inadequate infrastructure could deter domestic investment [134] as well as foreign direct investment (FDI) [135]. Access to roads and water were important to develop economically the regions in Kenya [136].

Based on an augmented Solow economic growth model, [69] presented pooled ordinary least square (OLS) growth regressions to test a variety of infrastructure indicators. They found that while roads, power, and telecommunication contributed significantly to long-term growth in the continent, other infrastructure such as water and sanitation had no impact. An alternative approach, such as in [137], used panel data. [138] focused on the sub-Saharan African (SSA) countries, a region that lacks public infrastructure. They found that infrastructure spending in the region contributed to economic growth, especially in less-developed economies. In addition to the growth model, a computable general equilibrium (CGE) has also been used. This approach made use of a large system of equations. These equations describe the behaviors of all economic agents (i.e. firms, households, government) and the linkages within the agents (e.g. inter-industry relationship) and between the agents. Therefore, this type of model is capable of assessing the economy-wide effects of various scenarios pertaining to infrastructure and public investment. Moreover, it can investigate the impacts of investment not only on economic growth but also on all variables related to economic output, such as factor income, international trade, and public expenditure via the interactions of the economic agents in response to investment shocks. And finally, the CGE approach enables us to simulate the impacts of infrastructure quality. For instance, [139] found a positive impact of infrastructure investment on well-being in the Limpopo Province in South Africa.

Other studies focused on individual countries, especially Nigeria and South Africa thanks to their high-quality data. [140] provided a framework to assess the efficiency of infrastructure investment across different regions in Nigeria. This framework yielded the marginal physical products of installed infrastructure, which helps the social planner to prioritize investment between regions. [141] explores the effects of infrastructure investment in South Africa and finds bidirectional effects. This result was confirmed by [2] with a detailed long-run database. In [142], the impact of household electrification on employment in South Africa's rural labor markets was investigated and found that electrification had significantly raised female employment within five years. This effect can be explained by the release of women from home production and the enabling of microenterprises.

4.6 The Relationship between Time and the Well-Being of the Households

As we aim to establish the impacts of travel time on household wealth, it is important to understand how time is discussed as a crucial component of the well-being of a household in the literature. Up to the 1960s, households did not appear prominently in formal economic discussions. Only a few works mentioned them in their analysis. [143] compared the efficiency of firms in producing goods for the market to the inefficiency of households in producing domestic services. Some researchers suggested that household production should have been included in the GNP [144].

It all changed with Becker in 1965 [145]. In his seminal work, households featured prominently on both the production and consumption sides. In particular, households combined their time and a bundle of goods to produce outputs such as food and childcare. At the same time, they also consumed these goods. With the formal presence of households in the analytical framework, time plays an important role in determining the wealth of the households. Goods can be consumed in different time periods [146]. When members of the households made education or job training decisions, forgone earnings due to time spent in education or training were much more important than tuition or fees ([147], [148], [149], [150], [151], [152]).

In Becker's model, a household produced a vector of commodities (e.g. childcare, leisure, etc.) with some goods and time. These goods entered the utility function separately. Time could be a vector with different components (e.g. weekdays and weekends, days and nights). Each component could have a different price. Facing a budget constraint, the household needed to choose the level of consumption for each good and the time allocated to each activity to maximize its utility. Time reduction for each activity (e.g. travel time) was considered to be a cost reduction, hence improving the utility and wealth of the household.

Inspired by Becker's model, new literature on home production emerged. [153] formalized human capital as a good that can be produced. The production function or technology depended on the individual's abilities, the quality of relevant inputs, and the setup of the institutions in which the households lived. This function would determine the optimal investment and hence provided insights into how households allocated time and their life-cycle wealth. [154] then extended [153]'s model to investigate how parents spent time as investments in their children. The human capital stock and the household's income were outcomes of the functional system that took into account the investments of the households at various stages of the children's life (preschool, in school, and post-school) and different places (home vs. school). The skills of the children could be drawn over time, as in [155]. Allocating time between children resulted in a trade-off between the quantity and the quality of the children in the household [156].

The idea of how time is a strong determinant of well-being was formulated comprehensively in [157]. Central to this work is the idea that the ultimate constraints that governed the individual wealth were the availability of human time, and the set of factors that determine how effectively time is used. Human time could be allocated to various activities. An individual could spend time working or producing goods and services (for household consumption). Time could be used in nonmarket production such as housework and childcare. Moreover, these activities required the individuals to be in a well-maintained physical state, which again required time-consuming work (e.g. eating and sleeping). As an input to these activities, time could be complementary to other inputs. For instance, time spent preparing a meal with a HelloFresh prepared meal kit would produce more outputs per unit of time than preparing the same meal without the help of HelloFresh. They concluded that time was as essential as other inputs, such as capital stocks, in the determination of a household's income and well-being.

Leisure is another example of how time is spent by households. Reading a book or socializing with friends are time-consuming activities that individuals might enjoy. Studying time-use surveys in the United States from 1965 to 2003, [158] found that people spent increasingly more time on leisure activities. The rise was significant, equivalent to five to ten weeks of vacation annually.

A related study to ours is [159], who showed the value of saved travel time. Applying [145]'s insight on the price of time, Gronau brought the discussion to individuals' decisions on the modes of transportation. Different from previous studies in the literature that considered time as a factor that affected abstract terms such as tastes, comfort, and utility, Gronau developed an analytical framework that showed us how to analyze time as a factor that affected the price of goods, in this case, the trips. Because time was a scarce resource, people valued time highly and any transport modes that saved time would be priced higher. He also showed that the price of time varied between different people. More precisely, any person would value their time approximately equal to their earnings. This had important implications on passenger demand for transportation. It helped transport service providers not only to price their existing products but also to think about future modes of transport that responded to travelers' need to save time.

5 Data

5.1 The Demographic and Health Surveys Dataset

In 1984, the United States Agency for International Development (USAID) set up the Demographic and Health Surveys Program. Being the successor of the World Fertility Survey and the Contraceptive Prevalence Survey projects, it aimed to help conduct more than 300 surveys in over 90 countries. This program has a variety of questionnaires, including the Man's questionnaire and the Woman's questionnaire.

In our project, we relied on the Household's questionnaire. The households were chosen across all ten Ghanaian regions, namely Greater Accra, Ashanti, Central, Eastern, Western, Volta, Bono, Northern, Upper-East, and Upper-West regions (see Figure 1). In this questionnaire, we extracted the household characteristics, including size (e.g. the number of members and the number of children), assets (e.g. cars/trucks), financial status (e.g. having access to a bank account), and the residential type (rural or urban). These characteristics reflected the household situation in 2016. More importantly, it yielded the level of wealth of the household which was our main measure of welfare. It is a composite index of wealth based on the possession of selected assets. This measure has several advantages over other measures that reflect the economic situation of the households such as income or consumption/expenditures. Indeed, because of the observability of the assets, this measure is more reliable and less subject to measurement errors. It is also less costly, which allows coverage of a large number of respondents. However, we have to be aware of its limitations. For instance, because of the normalization of the index, the absolute value has little meaning. We can only make a statement about the growth of the wealth index but not the index itself. Moreover, extending the analysis with the indices from different countries or continents could be problematic [160].

Table 2 presents the description of the information extracted from this dataset.

Figure 4 shows the wealth index of different regions in Ghana in 2003.[3] The wealth index ranges from 1 (poorest) to 5 (richest) with darker colors indicating higher values. The aerial map highlights that households in the south are wealthier than those in the north. The capital region, Greater Accra, is home to a significant number of wealthy households, followed by the Ashanti, Central, Eastern and Western regions. The Upper West, Upper East, and Northern Regions are home to the poorest households as of 2003.

Figure 5 illustrates the evolution of the wealth index from 2003 to 2016.[4] The wealth index changes were calculated as the changes in the log terms of the regional wealth index values. The changes range from −1.5 to 1 with darker colors corresponding to larger positive changes. An interesting fact emerges here. Being the home to most of the economic activities and population in Ghana, the South received relatively more infrastructure investment than the North did. Figure 5 also shows that more remarkable changes in the wealth

---

[3] We draw this map by merging the aerial regional map, obtained from the [197] database, and our DHS Covariate Database. We then used Rstudio to plot geospatial maps. Spatial manipulation was undertaken using the sf (special feature) and ggplot2 (grammar of graphics declarative creative system) packages. In consideration of the time-variant nature of the data due to the regional referendum on December 27, 2018, that created six new regions, this analysis is conducted based on the ten Ghanaian regions recognized before the referendum.

[4] To draw this figure, we followed the same process as described in Footnote 2.

Table 2 The DHS survey

Variables	Description
Cluster number	Each location in the sample is assigned a cluster number by DHS agents. It serves as a unique spatial (locational) identifier for households (respondents) within the country, allowing for a better understanding of strategic locations.
Household number	Each household that resides within a given sample point or cluster is assigned a numeric identifier.
Place type	Place type is a variable that classifies a household as in either a rural or urban area. The DHS dataset classifies urban areas into large cities, small cities, and towns. Large cities are cities with a population of over one million. Small cities are cities with a population of over fifty thousand but fewer than one million. Towns are other urban areas that fall outside the classification of the aforementioned cities. Rural areas, on the other hand, are areas in the countryside. An urban place type is denoted by 1, and a rural place type is denoted by 0 in the dataset. This provides an additional informational factor to identify whether one's residential place type plays a significant role concerning wealth development.
Number of household members	The number of household members variable refers to the total number of people who reside within that household and that can be classified as members. A household with a larger number of members may require more expenditure. As a result, household size could have a significant impact on estimated household wealth.

Table 2 (cont.)

Variables	Description
Number of children	This variable refers to the number of dependent children living in that household. Similar to the number of household members, the number of children living in the household is an important factor that determines the level of expenditure, and hence the estimated wealth of the household.
Sex of the head of the household	This variable indicates the gender of the lead breadwinner of the household. It takes the value 1 if this person is male and 0 otherwise. There is evidence that the gender of the household head is an important characteristic of the household, especially in developing countries like Ghana ([161], [162]).
Age of the head of household	The age of the head of the household could potentially have an impact on the wealth of the household as an older head of household may have had more time to accumulate and acquire wealth in comparison to a relatively younger head of household.
Number of bedrooms	The number of bedrooms can serve as a proxy for the size of the house. It can be an indicator of the wealth of the household.
Vehicle possession	The possession of a vehicle (whether a car or a truck) is an indicator of household wealth because such a vehicle is an important household asset.
Bank account	A dummy variable of whether the household has a bank account. In other words, it indicates whether the household has access to financial services. The literature provides some evidence of how financial inclusion is an important determinant of the household's wealth ([163], [164]).

Wealth Index

The wealth index is our main economic outcome. It is a composite measure of a household's cumulative living standard. The DHS estimated the index using data on a household's ownership of selected assets, such as televisions and bicycles; materials used for housing construction; and types of water access and sanitation facilities [165]. The estimation was carried out as follows. The wealth index situated households on a continuous scale of relative wealth, created with the principal components analysis statistical method. More precisely, the households in the interviews were divided into five quintiles of wealth to cross-examine the influence of wealth on different health, nutrition, and population indicators. The five wealth quintiles were then categorized from 1 to 5 with the poorest households in category 1 and the richest ones in category 5. In our dataset, the wealth index was reported for the years 2003, 2016, 2017, and 2019.

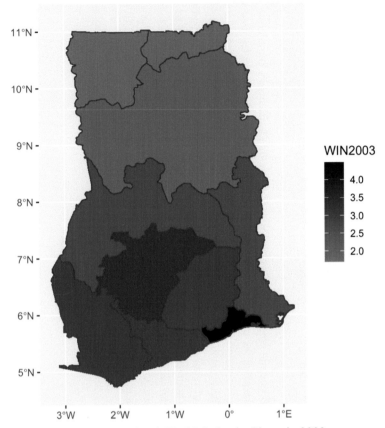

Figure 4 Regional Wealth Index in Ghana in 2003
WIN: Wealth Index

index took place in this region. The regions that experienced the most wealth enhancement were the Central, Oti and Volta (see Figure 1). By contrast, the Savannah region and the North suffered large drops in wealth.

5.2 The DHS Geospatial Covariate Datasets

In the household questionnaire, each household's location was identified by a cluster with the longitude and latitude coordinates. This information allows us to merge the DHS with the second dataset, namely the Geospatial Covariate dataset. This second dataset serves two purposes. First, it allows us to measure the "output" of infrastructure development in Ghana. In particular, it has statistics on the time residents took to travel to a large settlement within their area. If the infrastructure was improved, this travel time would be reduced significantly. The second purpose of this dataset is to provide a measure of the natural conditions at the disaggregated level. These conditions are perfect instruments for travel time because they are

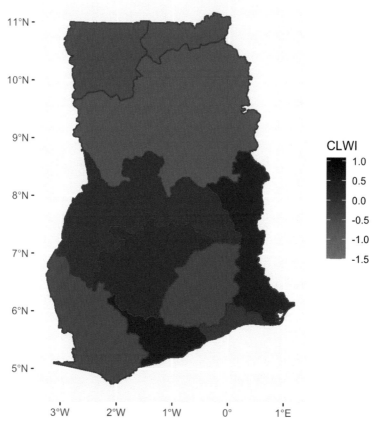

Figure 5 Changes in Wealth Index from 2003 to 2016
CLWI: Changes (in log term) in Wealth index

strongly related to travel time and, as we will later show, are largely exogenous. In other words, they provide us with a quasi-natural experiment to investigate the impact of infrastructure development, via travel time reduction. Table 3 presents the description of all the variables from this covariate dataset that we use.

The travel time to a metropolitan area in 2000 was displayed in Figure 6.[5] The lighter colors indicate shorter travel times. The regions with the longest travel time were the Eastern, the Western, and the Western North. The regions that were closest to metropolitan areas were the Ashanti, the Central, and the Greater Accra, which were located in the South (see Figure 1).

Figure 7 reports the changes in travel time from 2000 to 2015.[6] In all regions, it took less time to travel to a metropolitan area in 2015 than in 2000. Regions in

---

[5] To draw this figure, we followed the same process as described in footnote 1.
[6] To draw this figure, we followed the same process as described in footnote 1.

Table 3 The DHS covariate datasets

Variables	Description
Travel time in 2000	This travel time was defined as the time in minutes needed to travel to the nearest metropolitan area. A metropolitan area is a location with a population of fifty thousand or more people based on infrastructural data in 2000 [166]. The population was counted by the number of people living within 2 kilometers for an urban area or within 10 kilometers for a rural buffer surrounding a DHS survey cluster location, based on infrastructure data in 2000. Travel times, also referred to as accessibility estimates, give us a measure of the level at which national transportation systems are connected and the degree to which regions are urban or rural. Indeed, areas that are closer to major roads will be relatively more connected even when they are at long distances from big cities [167].
Travel time in 2015	Similar to travel time in 2000, the travel time in 2015 measures the average time in minutes it took household members to travel to a metropolitan area [166]. Interestingly, the new estimates in 2015 took into account data on recent expansion in infrastructure networks, particularly in lower-resource settings, which are provided in unprecedented detail and precision by OpenStreetMap and Google. It was a collaborative work between the University of Oxford's Malaria Atlas Project (MAP), Google, the EU Joint Research Center (JRC), and the University of Twente [168]. Using such data, the MAP developed a global accessibility estimate that quantifies travel time to cities. It does so by integrating ten global-scale surfaces that affect human movement rates and 13,840 high-density urban centers within an established geospatial-modeling framework.

Length of the growing season	It refers to the number of days in a year when the temperature is above 5°C and moisture conditions are considered adequate for crop growth. The variable is reported in one of sixteen categories within the 2-kilometer (urban) or 10-kilometer (rural) area surrounding the clusters in the DHS survey. Under rain-fed conditions, the beginning of the growing period is linked to the start of the rainy season. The growing period for most crops continues beyond the rainy season and, to a greater or lesser extent, crops mature on moisture stored in the soil profile. The sixteen categories are 1 (0 days); 2 (1–29 days); 3 (30–59 days); 4 (60–89 days); 5 (90–119 days); 6 (120–149 days); 7 (150–179 days); 8 (180–209 days); 9 (210–239 days); 10 (240–269 days); 11(270–299 days); 12 (300–329 days);13 (330–364 days); 14 (less than 365 days); 15 (365 days); 16 (more than 365 days). As a result, this variable is treated as a scale variable in our analysis.
Slope	This variable measures roughness of the terrain around a DHS cluster. It was derived by processing the United States Geological Survey GTOPO30 digital elevation model with the ArcMap 10.5.0 slope tool [169].

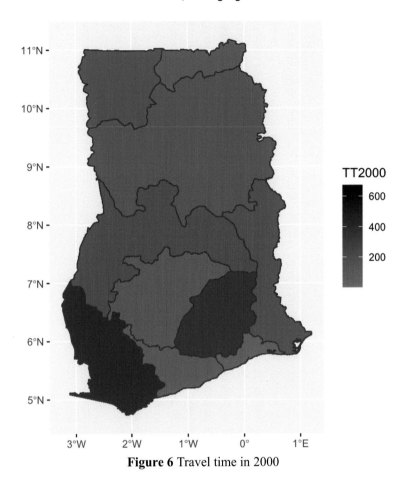

Figure 6 Travel time in 2000

dark colors enjoyed the highest reduction in travel time. They were the Western North and the Western (Figure 1).

6 Research Methodology

6.1 Theoretical Framework

The central theme of our analysis is the impacts of infrastructure, proxied by travel time reduction, on economic development, measured via the wealth index. To prove this hypothesis, we need to establish time as a component of wealth. In other words, like other conventional assets such as houses and cars, time must have a price. We borrow the framework from [159]. In his framework, a household is a producer of many activities $Z_i, i = 1, \ldots, n$. The production function for each activity i combines some market inputs X_i, and the time involved T_i. For instance,

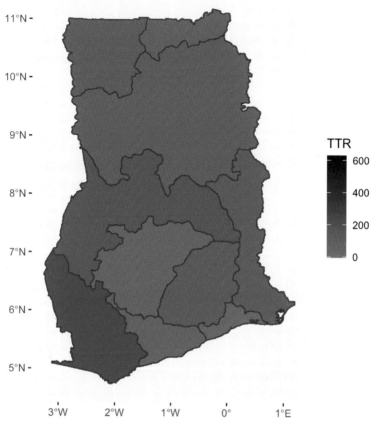

Figure 7 Changes in travel time from 2000 to 2015

watching a movie requires not only the watching time but also a subscription to the streaming services such as Netflix, Disney+, or Prime Video. Another example is childcare, which requires the time spent with the children and inputs such as toys and books. More specifically, the production of activity i can be represented as follows:

$$Z_{i,} = f_i(X_{i,} T_i). \tag{1}$$

Note that the technology for each activity can be different, denoted by the subscript i. A special activity that the household performs is work because it brings income to the household. To distinguish this activity from other activities, we use the subscript ω. Each activity yields some value to the household. Therefore, the objective of the households is to choose the level of each activity to maximize its utility:

$$U\left(Z_{1,\dots,}Z_n,Z_\omega\right). \tag{2}$$

The household faces two constraints. First, the budget constraint states that the amount of money spent on the inputs cannot be greater than the income generated from the household's work:

$$\sum_{i=1}^{n} P_i * X_i + P_\omega * X_\omega \leq W(Z_\omega). \tag{3}$$

Second, the time constraint states that the sum of the time spent on all activities cannot be greater than the total time available to the household (e.g. 24 hours a day):

$$\sum_{i=1}^{n} T_i + T_\omega \leq T. \tag{4}$$

To solve its problem, we need to set up the Lagrangian:

$$\mathcal{L} = U\left(Z_{1,\dots,}Z_n,Z_\omega\right) + \lambda *(W(Z_\omega) - \sum_{i=1}^{n}(P_i * X_i + P_\omega * X_\omega))$$

$$+ \mu *(T - \sum_{i=1}^{n}(T_i + T_\omega)). \tag{5}$$

Differentiating the Lagrangian $\mathcal{L}$ with respect to work Z_ω yields:

$$\frac{\partial \mathcal{L}}{\partial Z_\omega} = \frac{\partial U}{\partial Z_\omega} + \lambda *\left(\frac{\partial W(Z_\omega)}{\partial Z_\omega} - P_\omega * \frac{\partial X_\omega}{\partial Z_\omega}\right) - \mu * \frac{\partial T_\omega}{\partial Z_\omega}$$

$$= u_\omega + \lambda * \omega - \mu * \frac{\partial T_\omega}{\partial Z_\omega} \tag{6}$$

In Equation 6, $\omega = \frac{\partial W(Z_\omega)}{\partial Z_\omega} - P_\omega * \frac{\partial X_\omega}{\partial Z_\omega}$ is the net marginal wage rate. Indeed, it is the marginal wage rate from work $\frac{\partial W(Z_\omega)}{\partial Z_\omega}$ minus the marginal cost of work (which is the marginal cost of the input X_ω associated with work). If we normalize work so that $\frac{\partial T_\omega}{\partial Z_\omega} = 1$ then we have:

$$\mu = u_\omega + \lambda * \omega. \tag{7}$$

Note that the Lagrangian multiplier μ measures the increase in the objective function that is obtained through a marginal relaxation in the time constraint. As a result, it is the marginal utility of time. Similarly, the Lagrangian λ measures the increase in the objective function that is obtained through a marginal relaxation in the budget constraint. Therefore, it is the marginal utility of income. The ratio between these two multipliers is the shadow price of time $K = \frac{\mu}{\lambda}$. From Equation 7 we have:

$$K = w + \frac{u_\omega}{\lambda}. \tag{8}$$

Equation 8 shows that the price of time depends on three factors. The first factor is the net marginal wage rate w. A person who has high earnings would value his(her) time higher than others. The second factor is the person's taste for work. If he(she) enjoys work ($u_\omega > 0$), the opportunity cost of other activities in terms of time would be high. Finally, the price of time depends on the marginal utility of income. An implication from Equation 8 is that the price of time only equals the marginal earnings if the household has no utility or dis-utility from work (i.e. when $u_\omega = 0$).

6.2 Empirical Strategy

In the previous section, we have established the price of time as a function of the wage rate and personal preferences. As a result, time can be considered an asset, like any durable good. In other words, time is a component of the household's wealth. More precisely, we can write wealth W as a function of all the assets $Y_i, i = 1, \ldots, m$ and time T:

$$W = f_i(Y_1, Y_2, \ldots Y_1, T). \tag{9}$$

The possession of time is very much similar to the possession of any other asset. Therefore, a reduction of travel time, which implies more time for other activities, improves the wealth of the household. Note that our main economic outcome is the wealth index which is calculated based on the possession of selected assets. Therefore, taking the log of Equation 9 and calculating the change in time yield:

$$\Delta w_i = \beta_0 + \beta_1 * \Delta t_i + \beta_2 * X_i + \varepsilon_i. \tag{10}$$

In Equation 10, w_i is the log of the welfare index of the household i, t_i is the log of the travel time reduction from the household location to the center of a city with a population of more than fifty thousand. The term Δ indicates the change of the values from 2000 to 2015 for time and from 2003 to 2016 for the wealth index. More specifically, Δw_i is the change in (the log of) the wealth index from 2003 to 2016 while Δt_i is the reduction of (the log of) the travel time from 2000 to 2015.

To rule out the confounding factors that might affect the household's welfare, we include a vector of controls X_i that contains the household characteristics. These characteristics are the number of household members and children, the gender of the household head, the type of residence, the possession of a vehicle, access to bank accounts, and the number of bedrooms.

The coefficient of interest is β_1, which indicates how the reduction of travel time would affect household wealth. The sign of this coefficient informs the direction of the effect. Its magnitude would help us to quantify the impact. The simplest technique to estimate this coefficient is the OLS regression.

A necessary condition for the use of the OLS regression is the exogeneity of the independent variables. In other words, the independent variables must be uncorrelated to the error terms. There is, however, reasonable doubt that it is the case, especially in our context. There are essentially three main ways in which endogeneity arises [21]. First, some variables that affect both the dependent and independent variables are omitted due to data unavailability. Second, there are *systematic* errors in measuring the independent variables. In particular, if the errors are related to the explanatory variables, then the OLS estimates will be biased. And lastly, one of the independent variables may be a function of the dependent variable. In our context, for example, it is possible that wealthy households use less time-consuming transportation modes.

In our view, the first problem is particularly pertinent for two reasons. First, we can find several variables for which data are not available. For instance, wealthy people tend to live in the suburbs, further from city centers. Therefore, more wealth can lead to a small reduction in travel time. At the same time, those people are more likely to see their wealth increase via their investment in education and the many other investment opportunities that less affluent people do not have. We will test this hypothesis in the subsequent section. Second, the way we construct our independent variable makes the last two concerns about endogeneity less likely. There is no obvious reason to believe that errors in measuring travel time are related to other explanatory variables. Note that the travel time is measured in the second dataset (the DHS covariates) while the other explanatory variables are collected from the first DHS dataset. These datasets were constructed independently. Moreover, it is unlikely that the reduction in travel time in 2015 was the result of the changes in wealth in later years.

There are several techniques to address this endogeneity issue. We can use the fixed effects to control for omitted variables ([170], [171]). However, this technique does not address the other problems of endogeneity, namely the simultaneity and reverse causality. Theoretically, the problems of simultaneity and reverse causality can be dealt with by the structural estimation. This type of technique employs multiple equations that jointly determine the production function and infrastructure investment. Examples of the application of this technique are in [172] and [173]. In [172], the institutional factors were key in determining infrastructure investment, while in [173] it was the political factors. In both papers, infrastructure was shown to contribute significantly to national production. However, this type of technique is both data demanding and econometrically challenging.

Other studies applied the generalized method of moments (GMM) that was introduced by [174] and later developed by [175]. A special case of the GMM technique is the IV method, the idea of which is to find instruments for the independent variable (travel time reduction) that satisfy two conditions:

i. The relevance condition: the instruments must be strongly correlated with the independent variable.

ii. The exclusion restriction condition: the instruments cannot suffer from the same problem as does the independent variable (i.e. they must be exogenous). In other words, they cannot be related to the error terms.

Finding the instruments to satisfy these conditions is often a challenging task. In our context, our prime candidate is the length of the growing season. It is a weather-dependent variable and, hence, satisfies the exclusion restriction condition. Moreover, it reflects the geographical conditions across different parts of Ghana. Therefore, it is relevant to the travel time in the regions. We also consider another candidate, terrain roughness (the slope). Similar to the length of the growing season, this candidate satisfies both conditions for an instrument, namely relevance and the exclusion restriction conditions.

With an instrument Z_i, in the first stage we regress our main regressor Δt_i on Z_i and other regressors:

$$\Delta t_i = \alpha_0 + \alpha_1 * \Delta t_i + \alpha_2 * Z_i + u_{it}. \tag{11}$$

Then in the second stage, we replace Δt_i in Equation 10 with the estimated $\widehat{\Delta t_i}$ from Equation 11. This approach is, hence, also called the two-stage least square (2SLS).

7 Empirical Results

7.1 The Ordinary Least Square Approach

Table 4 presents the results. In Column 1, we estimated Equation 10 using the OLS method. It is no surprise that households that can afford to buy vehicles or large houses experienced a large rise in wealth. Indeed, if the household possessed a vehicle by the time of the survey (i.e. 2016), either a car or a truck, their wealth

Table 4 Impacts of travel time reduction

	OLS	IV	
		First stage result	Second stage result
	(1)	(2)	(3)
Dependent variable:	Δ ln(Wealth index)	Δ ln(Travel time reduction)	Δ ln(Wealth index)
Δ Ln(Travel time reduction)	0.009*		0.118***
	(0.005)		(0.031)
Vehicle possession	0.310***	0.47***	0.262***
	(0.025)	(0.08)	(0.030)
Number of household members	−0.031***	−0.024**	−0.029***
	(0.004)	(0.011)	(0.004)
Number of children	0.015	0.014	0.014
	(0.009)	(0.028)	(0.010)
Household head gender	−0.013	0.025	−0.015
	(0.013)	(0.040)	(0.014)
Urban residents	0.363***	1.04***	0.249***
	(0.014)	(0.039)	(0.035)

	(1)	(2)	(3)
Bank Account	0.394***	0.145***	0.379***
	(0.012)	(0.038)	(0.014)
Number of Bedrooms	0.046***	0.029	0.042***
	(0.006)	(0.02)	(0.007)
Changes in the length of the growing season		0.0015***	
		(0.0001)	
No. Observations	4,446	4,446	4,446
Adjusted R-squared	0.426	0.359	0.359

Note: The dependent variable is the change in log terms of the wealth index between 2003 and 2016.
The key regressor is the change in log terms of the travel time between 2000 and 2015. Data were collected from the DHS and the DHS Geospatial Covariate Database. Standard errors are in parentheses. * $p < 0.1$, ** $p < 0.05$, *** $p < 0.01$

would increase by 31 percent more. And each additional bedroom would raise wealth by a further 5 percent.

The structure of the households could play an important role here. Large households tended to struggle to grow wealth. We find that having one extra household member reduced wealth by 3 percent. Households with children could be credit-constrained and therefore unable to accumulate wealth [176]. However, here we find no evidence of the impact of the number of children on a household's wealth. Using a similar dataset as ours in Pakistan, [177] suggests that the wealth index could depend on the gender of the head of the household. In particular, male-headed households are more likely to have a lower wealth index than households headed by a female. We find no such evidence in Ghana.

The type of residence was shown to affect the wealth accumulation process. Our estimates show that living in urban areas would add 36 percent to the rise in wealth from 2003 to 2016 in Ghana. It is consistent with other studies in the literature. For instance, [178] finds a large urban–rural gap in terms of housing wealth. This was because of the faster rise in values of housing in urban areas, due to the hukou system and the disparity in educational opportunities, job availability, and positional wages between the large cities and peripheral areas.[7] Most people in developing countries do not have access to financial services. The average coverage was only 26 percent, compared to 90 percent in most OECD countries [163]. The use of these services is even more worrying. In the case of Ghana, according to the Living Standard Measurement Study, only 3 percent of households used formal institutions to borrow in 1998 [179] Our estimates suggest that having a bank account would increase household wealth by a further 39 percent. This is consistent with the literature. Indeed, finance development would reduce inequality and provide opportunities for all ([180], [181]), and enhance productivity [182] and profitability [183]. As a result, countries with more developed financial systems tend to grow faster [184].

A study similar to ours showed that families with bank accounts in the United States were more likely to have more income, business ownership, and real estate wealth [164].

The coefficient of interest is that of travel time reduction. The estimate by the OLS method shows that travel time reduction did enhance the wealth of the residents. The coefficient of this variable is significantly positive at the 90 percent confidence level. However, the magnitude of this wealth change was

---

[7] The hukou in China serves as a local passport. People who do not have hukou do not have access to local facilities such as public schools and hospitals. They also do not benefit from local government support such as access to the housing provident fund or a pension scheme.

quite small. A 10 percent travel reduction only enhanced household wealth by 0.09 percent.

The small estimated effect of travel time reduction should not be a surprise. Indeed, it is very likely that this regressor is endogenous. In this case, the necessary condition of the OLS method, which is that the independent variables must be uncorrelated to all the error terms, is violated. This problem arises when some explanatory variables are omitted. An example is the starting wealth of the household. Affluent households would likely choose to live in suburbs. For instance, [185] show that the percentage of poor people in American cities was high (19 percent) compared to that in the suburbs (only 7.5 percent). As a result of preferring to live in the suburbs, rich people's travel time to a metropolitan area from their home would be unlikely to be reduced. At the same time, they would have more opportunities to increase their wealth compared to less affluent households. Lower travel time reduction and higher wealth increase for rich people results in a negative correlation between the error terms and our main regression, which means we would have a negative bias here. In other words, the coefficient of travel time reduction would be underestimated, which explains the small magnitude of the effect. A solution for this problem is to use the instrumental variable approach.

7.2 Instrumental Variable Approach

The instrumental variable approach consists of two steps. First, we need to find an instrument; then we apply the 2SLS estimation. Intuitively, in the first stage, we regress our endogenous regressor, which is the travel time reduction, on the instrument that we have found in the first step and on the other regressors. In the second stage, we replace the endogenous regressor in the main regression equation with the value estimated in the first stage.

The instrument that we need to find must satisfy two conditions. First, it must be a good predictor of our main regressor (i.e. the travel time reduction). At the same time, it cannot be correlated with the error terms. A candidate is the length of the growing season, which reflects the change in the number of rainy days. Indeed, Ghana experiences significant flooding due to heavy rainfall every year. Heavy rainfalls coupled with poor road quality and ineffective road drainage have resulted in floods over the years. One of the most impactful flooding episodes occurred in the capital city, Accra, on June 3, 2015 (dubbed the June 3rd Disaster) [186]. It caused over 150 deaths; emergency services were spread thin and faced mobility difficulties. Flooding in Ghana has been an annually recurring problem. More recently, over 100 homes, major roads, and bridges were destroyed, with about 1,605 people affected in the Upper West region of Ghana on August 19, 2021. Five fatalities were reported after flooding in the Northern region on the 26th and 28th of August 2021 [187]. Days of heavy rainfall caused deadly flash floods in the Ashanti region, with 5 dead and over 200 people displaced after their homes were damaged in June 2021 [187]. The Ashanti region saw similar instances in September 2020 and October 2019. Heavy rainfall on October 10, 2020, also generated flash floods, leading to traffic chaos in Accra. Similar occurrences happened on June 8, 2020, and in October 2019, with other floods in the Eastern region in October 2019 [187]. These events point to the fact that rainfalls are strongly correlated with travel time. We use this fact to choose the length of the growing season as our instrument.

It is important to test the strength of our instrument. Recall that our instrument has to satisfy two conditions: it has to be uncorrelated with the error terms but correlated strongly with the endogenous variable. The first stage results are reported in Column 2 in Table 4. The coefficient of our instrument, which is the changes in the number of rainy days, is statistically significant at the 1-percent level, which indicates that our instrument is strong. Further test results are reported in Column 1 in Table 5. We can check the first condition with the overidentification test. The null

Table 5 Tests of instrumental variables

	(1)	(2)
Overidentification test		
Sargan statistics	0	0
Underidentification tests		
Anderson canon. corr. LM statistic	119.23	435.259
Weak identification tests		
Sanderson-Windmeijer multivariate F test of excluded instruments	122.27	481.52
Cragg-Donald Wald F statistic	122.27	481.52
Weak instrument–robust inference		
Anderson-Rubin Wald F test	16.34	0.07
Anderson-Rubin Wald test chi-square test	16.38	0.07
Stock-Wright LM S statistic	16.32	0.07

Note: We report the tests for our instruments. In Column 1, our instrument was the length of the growing season. In Column 2, our instrument was the slope of the territory.

hypothesis is that the instruments are valid (i.e. they are correlated with the error terms and that the excluded instruments are correctly excluded from the estimated equation). The Sargan statistics confirm that we cannot reject this hypothesis. Since we only have one endogenous variable, the second condition can be checked with the underidentification test. The null hypothesis of this test is that the model is underidentified. Rejecting this hypothesis would imply that the endogenous variable is just identified by our instrument. We test this hypothesis by applying the [188] canonical correlations test. The Lagrange multiplier (LM) statistic of this test is 119.23 which rejects the null hypothesis. Therefore, our tests confirm that the instrument satisfies both conditions.

We provide further tests to check the validity of our instrumental variable approach. The first test is whether our instrument is weakly correlated with the endogenous variable, using statistics from [189] and [190]. However, in our case, when there is only one endogenous variable, the two tests are identical. They both reject the null hypothesis that our instrument is weak. The second test is the significance of our endogenous regressors. In particular, the null hypothesis is that the coefficient of the endogenous regressor is 0. For this test, we provide 3 statistics. The first two statistics are the F-statistic and the chi-square statistic from [191]. They are 16.34 and 16.38, which reject the null hypothesis. This result is consistent with the LM S-statistic from [192].

These tests confirm the validity of our instrument variable approach. It is time to check how our main result changes with this approach. The second stage results of this approach are reported in Column 3 in Table 4. Relative to the OLS estimates in Column 1, two observations emerge. The coefficients of all of the exogenous regressors remain relatively unchanged, both statistically and economically. Vehicle possession, the number of household members, the number of bedrooms, whether the household lived in an urban area, and if they had a bank account all have coefficients that are statistically different from 0. Their magnitudes are close to the corresponding values in Column 1. In other words, the OLS and IV approaches provide consistent results regarding the other regressors. Recall that we move from the OLS to the IV method because of the endogeneity of our main regressor, the travel time reduction, which biases our estimate. Our analysis suggests that the bias is downward, which is confirmed by the new estimate. The coefficient of the travel time reduction is now more significant, both statistically and economically. Indeed, the statistical significance goes up from 90 percent to 99 percent. Moreover, the magnitude of the impact is much more pronounced. With the OLS estimates, a 10 percent reduction in travel time only resulted in a 0.09 percent increase in the wealth index. With the IV estimates, the impact jumped up by nearly thirteen times, to 1.2 percent.

8 Robustness Checks

In this section, we will test if our result is robust to a battery of specifications.

8.1 Controls for Regional Wealth Index

Note that in Equation 10, we control for several household characteristics: size of the household, the number of children living in the household, and the number of bedrooms. Financial situation, measured by access to banks and the possession of vehicles, is also included, as is type of household, whether in urban or rural areas, and whether the household is led by a male or a female. In other words, we take into account the possible household demographic factors that might affect its wealth. However, one might be concerned that regional attributes could also play a role. As we discussed in Section 3, the economic landscape in Ghana is divided by Lake Volta. Most of Ghana's economic activities are concentrated in the South. It is then plausible that the southern households have more wealth than their counterparts in the North.

To address this issue, we then add the regional wealth index in 2003 to control for this possible regional difference. Our regression specification can be rewritten as:

$$\Delta w_{ir} = \beta_0 + \beta_1 * \Delta t_{ir} + \beta_2 * X_{ir} + \beta_3 * W_{r2003} + \varepsilon_{ir}. \tag{12}$$

In Equation 12, the subscripts i and r indicate the household i in region r. In other words, w_{ir} is the log of the wealth index of household i in region r. The log of the travel time to the center of a city is t_{ir}. The household characteristics are embodied in the vector X_{ir}. The term Δ still indicates the changes from 2000 to 2015. We still instrument the travel time reduction by the length of the growing season to avoid the endogeneity problem.

The new control is the wealth index of region r in 2003 W_{r2003}. Our results are reported in Column 1 in Table 6. Relative to the IV estimates in Column 3 in Table 4, all of our coefficients remain unchanged. This confirms that our result is robust.

8.2 Fixed Effects

In Section 8.1, we control for the regional wealth index. However, there might be more regional attributes that affect household wealth. We cannot include all the attributes due to data availability. One solution is to add the regional fixed effect into our regression Equation 10. Specifically, our regression equation becomes:

$$\Delta w_{ir} = \beta_0 + \beta_1 * \Delta t_{ir} + \beta_2 * X_{ir} + v_r + \varepsilon_{ir}. \tag{13}$$

Table 6 Robustness checks

	(1)	(2)	(3)	(4)	(5)
ΔLn(travel time reduction)	0.112***	0.066	0.004	0.125***	0.354***
	(0.030)	(0.062)	(0.015)	(0.045)	(0.087)
Vehicle possession	0.298***	0.324***	0.312***	0.254***	0.277***
	(0.028)	(0.034)	(0.026)	(0.016)	(0.033)
Number of household members	−0.031***	−0.030***	−0.031***	−0.023***	
	(0.004)	(0.004)	(0.004)	(0.001)	
Number of children	0.013	0.015	0.015*		0.031***
	(0.009)	(0.009)	(0.009)		(0.011)
Household head gender	−0.032**	−0.021	−0.013		−0.001
	(0.014)	(0.014)	(0.013)		(0.016)
Urban residents	0.265***	0.317***	0.368***	0.305***	0.072
	(0.033)	(0.063)	(0.020)	(0.042)	(0.084)
Bank account	0.408***	0.402***	0.395***	0.421***	0.311***
	(0.013)	(0.013)	(0.012)	(0.006)	(0.018)

Table 6 (cont.)

	(1)	(2)	(3)	(4)	(5)
Number of bedrooms	0.029***	0.031***	0.046***	0.032***	0.019**
	(0.007)	(0.007)	(0.006)	(0.003)	(0.007)
No. Observations	4,446	4,446	4,446	20,570	4,373
Adjusted R-squared	0.386	0.43	0.426	0.419	0.0823

Note: The dependent variable is the change in log terms of the wealth index between 2003 and 2016.
The key regressor is the change in log terms of the travel time between 2000 and 2015. Data were collected from the Demographic and Health Survey (DHS) and the DHS Geospatial Covariate Database. In Column 1, we controlled for the regional wealth index. Region fixed effects were included in Column 2. In Column 3, we employed the slope of the territory, which indicates the roughness of the terrain, as an alternative instrument variable. In Column 4, the dependent variable is the change in log terms of the wealth index between 2003 and 2017, while in Column 5, the dependent variable is the change in log terms of the wealth index between 2003 and 2019. Standard errors are in parentheses. * $p < 0.1$, ** $p < 0.05$, *** $p < 0.01$

What differs between Equation 10 and Equation 13 is the presence of the fixed effect v_r. This fixed effect controls for all regional specific factors that might have been omitted. The factors can be (i) geographical, such as the location of the region; (ii) social, such as the population density; or (iii) economic, such as the development policies. We report the results in Column 2 in Table 6. Comparing these results with those in Columns 1 and 3 in Table 4, we observe that all the coefficients retain the same sign. This implies that the direction of our effects remains unchanged. Statistically and economically, all the coefficients except that of the travel time reduction are similar. Finally, the coefficient of the travel time reduction is economically more significant than that of the OLS estimate from Column 1 in Table 4, but less statistically and economically significant than that of the IV estimate in Column 3 in Table 4. That the coefficient is greater than that from the OLS regression is not surprising given that we still apply the IV method. The second result, that the coefficient has a smaller magnitude than that from Column 3 in Table 4 can be explained by the fact that controlling for more factors would reduce the significance of the impacts of our main regressor. These results suggest that even when we control for all the regional attributes, we still find evidence that travel time reduction did enhance the change in the wealth index of the households in Ghana.

8.3 A Different Instrument

We have shown that our main result, which is that the more travel time was reduced, the higher the increase in the wealth index of the households, is robust to the inclusion of additional controls. To bring more confidence to our result, we will test the robustness of our result against alternative measures of our main variables, namely the instrument and the dependent variable. In this section, we will look at an alternative instrument. Alternative measures of the wealth index will be employed for robustness tests in the next section.

One possible instrument that we consider is the slope of the territory. It indicates how rough the terrain around a cluster is. The data are taken from the United States Geological Survey GTOPO30 digital elevation model. Our assumption is that the roughness of the terrain is a natural indicator of the travel time that is not correlated with other factors that might affect the wealth index.

As with our main instrument, we first check the validity of the new instrument. The test results are provided in Column 2 in Table 5. We cannot reject the validity of this instrument. Indeed, the Anderson canonical correlation test rejects the null hypothesis that the model is underidentified. This suggests that our new instrument, which is the territorial slope is a valid instrument.

There are concerns regarding this instrument, however, in regard to its quality. Here our tests provide mixed results. On the one hand, the Sanderson–Windmeer test rejects the hypothesis that this instrument is a weak one. On the other hand, both the Anderson–Rubin and the Stock–Wright tests cannot reject the hypothesis that the coefficient of the endogenous regressor is 0.

We report the estimated results with the new instrument in Column 3 in Table 6. Again we find evidence that travel time reduction led to higher household's wealth. If the household could reach a metropolitan area in 10 percent less time, their wealth index would increase by 0.04 percent. In addition, all the other regressors have predicted impacts. Vehicle possession, living in the urban areas, having a bank account or more bedrooms all contributed positively to the wealth index. At the same time, the number of household members had an adverse effect on wealth. Finally, the coefficient of the travel time reduction is less significant, both statistically and economically, compared to the estimates with our prime instrument (see Column 3 in Table 4), which is a result of the low strength of this new instrument

8.4 A Different Wealth Index

In this section, we carry out the final robustness check with an alternative measure of the wealth index. Note that in our main specification, the term Δ is the difference between the values in 2003 and 2016. Therefore, what we have picked up might be the short-term effect of infrastructure. To measure the long-term effect, and to further confirm the robustness of our result, we then measure the change in the wealth index in later years. We report the results in Columns 4 and 5 in Table 6. More precisely, in Column 4, the dependent variable is the change in the log term of the wealth index between 2003 and 2017. In Column 5, we replace the wealth index in 2017 with that in 2019. Note that in 2017, we do not have data on the number of children and the gender of the household head. Similarly, in 2019, data on the number of household members is missing.

Once more, our results survive this robustness check. All the coefficients remain unchanged statistically and qualitatively. More interestingly, they reveal the long-term effect of infrastructure. A 10 percent reduction in the travel time would increase the wealth index by 12.5 percent in 2017, up from 11.8 percent in 2016 (see Column 4 in Table 6). The result in Column 5 when we measure the changes between 2003 and 2019 is even more striking. The effect rises to 35.4 percent, which is about three times the effect that we observe in the benchmark case.

9 Policy Implications and Conclusion

The findings in our analysis lead us to a variety of policy implications which we will present in this section.

9.1 Policy Implications

Evidence-based support for infrastructure-based development plans. In 2018, the GoG approved the LTNDP to guide the country's development over the next forty years. An integral part is the NIP which aims to provide significant funds to infrastructure projects. Such an ambitious plan needs to be supported by evidence. Our report provides quantitative estimates of how the reduction of travel time as a direct effect of these projects is translated into residents' wealth.

Fill the infrastructure investment gap. By 2040, the global infrastructure gap could be as much as $15 trillion. The need to fill this gap has never been greater given the disastrous impacts of the COVID-19 pandemic. Governments with a strong infrastructure system were better prepared to deal with the crisis. Our analysis shows that investments in infrastructure, which reduce transportation costs, will improve residents' wealth. It calls for large and transformative infrastructure programs to help recover the economy in Ghana in particular, and in developing countries in general.

Make the infrastructure investment inclusive. In the previous sections, we show that if we can reduce the travel time to a metropolitan area by 10 percent, the wealth index of a household in Ghana would increase by 1.2 percent. This result suggests that governments should make infrastructure investment in less-developed areas a priority in their economic development plan. Indeed, in the case of Ghana, regions in the North and Southwest were less developed (Figure 4) and less connected to the metropolitan areas (Figure 6). Our analysis suggests that investing in these peripheral areas will have a better return. This is because in these areas, transportation costs in terms of time and money are large. It will, therefore, be easier to reduce these barriers which leads to significant wealth improvement. In addition, this will lead to greater balance in the economy by bringing the remote and less-developed areas closer to the other parts of the country in terms of economic development.

Establish high-quality and transparent political institutions. The success of infrastructure investment depends crucially on the quality of the local and central governments which decide whether and how to spend public resources on new projects. It is suggested that these governments respond to political and individual interests rather than to economic efficiency [193]. This suggestion is supported by historical data [194]. Moreover, incumbents who seek to be reelected often select large-scale projects as highlights to attract voters' approval ([195], [196]).

To establish sound political institutions, transparent and clear guidelines must be set to approve and evaluate projects. Regions with weak, underdeveloped, and fewer institutions must receive regular monitoring and support. Strong coordination and a coherent plan at the national level are also needed to ensure the sustainability of the projects.

9.2 Conclusion

Infrastructure is the precondition for any development plan that aims to enhance the wealth and well-being of residents. At the basic level, people need access to electricity, water and other utilities. At a higher level, transport infrastructure such as highways and railroads are needed to ensure the economy in particular and the society, in general, can operate smoothly and efficiently.

The infrastructure investment gap has never been greater. The pre-COVID estimates were $15 trillion for the next twenty years [5]. This gap will continue to rise with the requirements from the economic recovery on the global stage after the end of the current pandemic. With the massive potential to be unlocked, Africa must be the hub for investment in the infrastructural sectors. Compared to other parts of the world, African countries lag in terms of filling the gap with only 57 percent of the demand for infrastructure being met.

We take Ghana as a prime case study because of its long-term development plans and the inadequate infrastructure system relative to its fast economic growth. In 2018, the government of Ghana issued the LTNDP to draw the development path for the country for the next forty years. The NIP is an integral part of this ambitious plan. This NIP responds to the need of improving the substandard infrastructure in Ghana. Our Element seeks to provide the empirical support for these long-term plans.

We have shown that investment in infrastructure can have quantitatively large impacts. Extending the road network and enhancing the quality of the transport system would bring the residents in the country closer to more developed areas with more opportunities for prosperity. Indeed, if the people in Ghana can get to these areas 10 percent faster, their wealth index could rise by 1.2 percent. Our analysis lends evidence-based support to the current development plans in the country. It calls for more investment in remote areas where the potential is enormous but is often overlooked in these plans.

This research was carried out during the COVID-19 pandemic. Because of the travel restrictions imposed by the governments to stop the spread of the virus, we were unable to collect further data for our investigation. Similar to [127], if we could get hold of the prices of commodities across different regions and time, we would be able to investigate the mechanism through which travel time reduction, thanks to the infrastructure investment from 2000 to 2015, enhanced the trade opportunities and people's welfare. This will be left for future research.

Abbreviations

2SLS	Two-stage least square approach
CGE	Computable general equilibrium
CIA	Central Intelligence Agency
DHS	The Demographic and Health Survey
FEED	Front-end engineering design
GIO	Global infrastructure outlook
GMM	Generalized method of moments
GoG	Government of Ghana
GPRTU	Ghana Private Road Transport Union
GQP	Golden Quadrilateral Program
GSS	Ghana Statistical Service
ICA	Infrastructure Consortium for Africa
IMF	International Monetary Fund
IV	Instrumental variable
LM	Lagrange multiplier
LTNDP	Long-Term National Development Plan
MOF	Ministry of Finance
MRH	Ministry of Roads and Highways
MRO	Maintenance, repair, and overhaul
NDPC	National Development Planning Commission
NIP	National Infrastructure Plan
OLS	Ordinary least square
TFP	Total factor productivity
USAID	United States Agency for International Development
WB	World Bank

References

[1] WorldBank. "Global Economic Prospect." 2022.

[2] P. Perkins, J. Fedderke, and J. Luiz. "An Analysis of Economic Infrastructure Investment in South Africa." *South African Journal of Economics* 72.2 (2005).

[3] FT. *UK Economic Rebound Leaves Output Far Below Pre-Pandemic Levels*. www.ft.com/content/dd35a8a5-a1e3-493b-a08b-787bfbcdd174. 2020.

[4] IMF. "After-Effects of the COVID-19 Pandemic: Prospects for Medium-Term Economic Damage." In *World Economic Outlook: Managing Divergent Recoveries*." International Monetary Fund, 2021, pp. 43–61.

[5] GIO. "Infrastructure Investment Need in the Compact with Africa countries." Global Infrastructure Outlook. 2018.

[6] CIA. "The World FactBook." Central Intelligence Agency. 2021.

[7] E. Boamah. "Accounting to the People." www.ndcmanchester.org/wp-content/uploads/2016/08/GREENBOOK ACCOUNTINGTOTHEPEOPLE .pdf. 2015.

[8] M. Arellano and S. Bond. "Some Tests of Specification for Panel Data: Monte Carlo Evidence and an Application to Employment Equations." *The Review of Economic Studies* 58.2 (1991), 277–97.

[9] D. Canning and M. Fay. "The Effect of Transportation Networks on Economic Growth." Columbia University mimeo. 1993.

[10] T. Deng. "Impacts of Transport Infrastructure on Productivity and Economic Growth: Recent Advances and Research Challenges." *Transport Reviews* 33.6 (2013), 686–99.

[11] R. Ford and P. Poret. "Infrastructure and Private Sector Productivity." OECD Working Paper No. 91. 1991.

[12] C. Hulten. "Infrastructure Capital and Economic Growth: How Well You Use It May be More Important than How Much You Have." NBER Working Paper No. 5847. 1996.

[13] N. Ismail and J. Mahyideen. "The Impact of Infrastructure on Trade and Economic Growth in Selected Asian Economies." ADBI Working Paper Series No. 553. 2015.

[14] D. Holtz-Eakin and A. Schwartz. "Infrastructure in a Structural Model of Economic Growth." *Regional Science and Urban Economics* 25.2 (1995), 131–51.

[15] I. Nadiri and T. Mamuneas. "Infrastructure and Public RD Investments and the Growth of Factor Productivity in US Manufacturing Industries." NBER Working Paper No. 4845. 1994.

[16] WorldBank. "Ghanas Infrastructure: A Continental Perspective." 2010.

[17] A. Banerjee, E. Dufloa, and N. Qian. "On the Road: Access to Transportation Infrastructure and Economic Growth in China." *Journal of Development Economics* 145 (2020). https://doi.org/10.1016/j.jdeveco.2020.102442.

[18] S. Gibbons, T. Lyytikäinen, H. Overman, and R. Sanchis-Guarner. "New Road Infrastructure: The Effects on Frms." *Journal of Urban Economics* 110 (2019), 35–50.

[19] L. Lenz, A. Munyehirwe, J. Peters, and M. Sievert. "Does Large-Scale Infrastructure Investment Alleviate Poverty? Impacts of Rwandas Electricity Access Roll-Out Program." *World Development* 89 (2017), 88–110.

[20] A. Munnell. "Infrastructure Investment and Economic Growth." *Journal of Economic Perspectives* 6.4 (1992), 189–98.

[21] J. Wooldridge. *Econometric Analysis of Cross Section and Panel Data.* MIT Press, 2010.

[22] GE. www.theglobaleconomy.com/rankings/seaportsquality/. The Global Economy. 2019.

[23] MRH. "2019 Annual Progress Report." Ministry of Roads and Highways. 2020.

[24] MRH. "Sector Medium-Term Development Plan (SMTDP): 2018–2021." Ministry of Roads and Highways. 2018.

[25] QZ. "Ghana's Plan to Build Sky Trains in Accra for 2.6 Billion USD Isn't Happening after All." https://qz.com/africa/2094653/ghanes-2–6-billion-skytrain-project-isnt-happening-after-all/. 2021.

[26] MRH. "Transport Sector Programme Support." Ministry of Roads and Highways. 2009.

[27] D. Owusu-Manu, A. Jehuri, D. J. Edwards, F. Boateng, and G. Asumadu. "The Impact of Infrastructure Development on Economic Growth in Sub-Saharan Africa with Special Focus on Ghana." *Journal of Financial Management of Property and Construction* 24.3 (2019), 253–73.

[28] MRH. "Review Report: Enhancing the Performance of Transport Sector for Trade and Regional Integration." Ministry of Roads and Highways. 2010.

[29] S. Densu, M. Salifu, and C. Attafuah. "Road User Safety on the National Highway 1 (N1-Highway) in Accra, Ghana." *The Journal of Civil and Environmental Research* 6.5 (2014), 136–42.

[30] E. Badu, D. Owusu-Manu, and D. Brown. "Barriers to the Implementation of Innovative Financing (IF) of Infrastructure." *Journal of Financial Management of Property and Construction* 17.3 (2012), 253–73.

[31] ICA. "Africa's Infrastructure: A Time for Transformation." World Bank and Infrastructure Consortium for Africa (ICA). 2010.

[32] ROG. *National Policy on Public Private Partnerships*. Ministry of Finance and Economic Planning, Government of Ghana. 1999.

[33] V. Foster and N. Pushak. "Ghana's Infrastructure: A Continental Perspective." World Bank Policy Research Working Paper No. 5600. 2011.

[34] R. Jedwab and R. Osei. "Structural Change in Ghana 1960–2010." George Washington University mimeo. 2012.

[35] MOF. *The 2017 Budget Statement and Economic Policy of the Government of Ghana for the 2017 Financial Year*. Ministry of Finance. 2017.

[36] CIA. "The World FactBook." Central Intelligence Agency. 2022.

[37] GSS. "Multidimensional Poverty – Ghana." Ghana Statistical Service. 2020.

[38] NDPC. "Long-Term National Development Plan for Ghana (2018–2057)." Progress Report to Parliament. 2016.

[39] J. Black, N. Hashimzade, and G. Myles. *A Dictionary of Economics*. Oxford University Press, 2017.

[40] J. Schumpeter. *The Theory of Economic Development*. Harvard Economic Studies. 1912.

[41] G. Meier. *Biography of a Subject: An Evolution of Development Economics*. Oxford University Press, 2005.

[42] K. Mandelbaum. *The Industrialisation of Backward Areas*. Blackwell, 1947.

[43] P. N. Rosenstein-Rodan. "Problems of Industrialisation of Eastern and South-Eastern Europe." *Economic Journal* 53 (1943), 202–11.

[44] D. Greenwald. *The McGraw Hill Dictionary of Modern Economics*. McGraw-Hill, 1965.

[45] A. Hirschman. *The Strategy of Economic Development*. Yale University Press, 1958.

[46] O. Bajo-Rubio and C. Diaz-Roldan. "Optimal Endowment of Public Capital: An Empirical Analysis for the Spanish Regions." *Regional Studies* 39.3 (2005), 297–304.

[47] M. Boarnet. "Infrastructure Services and the Productivity of Public Capital: The Case of Streets and Highways." *National Tax Journal* 50.1 (1997), 39–57.

[48] K. Duffy-Deno and R. Eberts. "Public Infrastructure and Regional Economic Development: A Simultaneous Equations Approach." *Journal of Urban Economics* 30.3 (1991), 329–43.

[49] A. Kemmerling and A. Stephan. "The Contribution of Local Public Infrastructure to Private Productivity and Its Political Economy: Evidence from a Panel of Large German Cities." *Public Choice* 113.3–4 (2002), 403–24.

[50] R. Krol. "The Role of Public Capital in the Economic Development Process." *International Journal of Public Administration* 24.10 (2001), 1041–60.

[51] C. Morrison and A. Schwartz. "State Infrastructure and Productive Performance." *American Economic Review* 86.5 (1996), 1095–11.

[52] F. Nourzad and M. Vrieze. "Public Capital Formation and Productivity Growth: Some International Evidence." *Journal of Productivity Analysis* 6.4 (1995), 283–95.

[53] R. Prud'homme. "Assessing the Role of Infrastructure in France by Means of Regionally Estimated Production Functions." *Infrastructure and the Complexity of Economic Development.* Springer-Verlag, 1996.

[54] M.D. Ramirez. "Public Capital Formation and Labour Productivity Growth in Mexico." *Atlantic Economic Journal* 30.4 (2002), 366–79.

[55] A. Stephan. "Assessing the Contribution of Public Capital to Private Production: Evidence from the German Manufacturing Sector." *International Review of Applied Economics* 17.4 (2003), 399–417.

[56] J. Sturm and J. De Haan. "Is Public Expenditure Really Productive: New Evidence for the USA and the Netherlands." *Economic Modelling* 12.1 (1995), 60–72.

[57] P. Wylie. "Infrastructure and Canadian Economic Growth 1946–1991." *The Canadian Journal of Economics* 29 (1996), S350–S355.

[58] L. Roller and L. Waverman. "Telecommunications Infrastructure and Economic Development: A Simultaneous Approach." *American Economic Review* 91.4 (2001), 909–23.

[59] N. Czernich, O. Falck, T. Kretschmer, and L. Woessmann. "Broadband Infrastructure and Economic Growth." *The Economic Journal* 121.552 (2011), 505–32.

[60] F. Nourzad. "The Productivity Effect of Government Capital in Developing and Industrialized Countries." *Applied Economics* 32.9 (2000), 1181–87.

[61] C. Calderon and A. Chong. "Volume and Quality of Infrastructure and The Distribution of Income: An Empirical Investigation." *Review of Income and Wealth* 50.1 (2004), 87–106.

[62] A. Alesina and R. Perotti. "Income Distribution, Political Instability and Investment." *American Economic Review* 40 (1996), 1202–29.

[63] D. Kaufmann, A. Kraay, and P. Zoido-Lobaton. "Governance Matters II: Update Governance Indicators for 2000–01." *The World Bank* (2002).

[64] C. Calderon and L. Serven. "Infrastructure and Economic Development in Sub-Saharan Africa." *Journal of African Economies* 19.1 (2010), 13–87.

[65] D. Holtz-Eakin. "Public Sector Capital and the Productivity Puzzle." *The Review of Economics and Statistics* 76.1 (1994), 11–21.

[66] M. Herrerias. "The Causal Relationship between Equipment Investment and Infrastructures on Economic Growth in China." *Frontiers of Economics in China* 5.4 (2010), 509–26.

[67] Y. Shi, S. Guo, and P. Sun. "The Role of Infrastructure in China's Regional Economic Growth." *Journal of Asian Economics* 49 (2017), 26–41.

[68] W. Zou, F. Zhang, Z. Zhuang and H. Song. "Transport Infrastructure, Growth, and Poverty Alleviation: Empirical Analysis of China." *Annals of Economics and Finance* 9.2 (2008), 345–71.

[69] B. Speciale Estache A. and D. Veredas. "How Much Does Infrastructure Matter to Growth in Sub-Saharan Africa?" World Bank Working Paper. 2005. www.researchgate.net/publication/228457801_How_Much_Does_ Infrastructure_Matter_to_Growth_in_Sub-Saharan_Africa

[70] V. German-Soto and H. Bustillos. "The Nexus between Infrastructure Investment and Economic Growth in the Mexican Urban Areas." *Modern Economy* 5.13 (2014), 1208–20.

[71] K. Arrow and M. Kurz. *Public Investment, the Rate of Return and Optimal Fiscal Policy*. The Johns Hopkins University, 1970.

[72] R. Barro. "Government Spending in a Simple Model of Exogenous Growth." *Journal of Political Economy* 98 (1990), 103–25.

[73] K. Futagami, Y. Morita, and A. Shibata. "Dynamic Analysis of an Endogenous Growth Model with Public Capital." *Scandinavian Journal of Economics* 95 (1993), 607–25.

[74] C. Tsoukis and N. Miller. "Public Services and Endogenous Growth." *Journal of Policy Modeling* 25 (2003), 297–307.

[75] S. Ghosh and U. Roy. "Fiscal Policy, Long-Run Growth, and Welfare in a Stockflow Model of Public Goods." *Canadian Journal of Economics* 37 (2004), 742–56.

[76] C. Hulten and R. Schwab. "Does Infrastructure Investment Increase the Productivity of Manufacturing Industry in the US?" In *Econometrics and the Cost of Capital: Essays in Honor of Dale Jorgenson*. Ed. by L. Lau. MIT Press, 2000, pp. 143–64.

[77] S. Bougheas, P. Demetriades, and T. Mamuneas. "Infrastructure, Specialization and Economic Growth." *Canadian Journal of Economics* 33.2 (2000), 506–22.

[78] P. Agenor. *Public Capital, Growth and Welfare*. Princeton University Press, 2013.

[79] S. Turnovsky. "Fiscal Policy, Adjustment Costs, and Endogenous Growth." *Oxford Economic Papers* 48 (1996), 361–81.

[80] P. Agenor. "Schooling and Public Capital in a Model of Endogenous Growth." *Economica* 78 (1996), 108–32.

[81] D. Aschauer. "Does Public Capital Crowd Out Private Capital?" *Journal of Monetary Economics* 24.2 (1989), 171–88.

[82] D. Aschauer. "Public Investment and Productivity Growth in the Group of Seven." *Economic Perspectives* 13.5 (1989), 17–25.

[83] P. David and J. Scadding. "Private Savings: Ultrarationality, Aggregation, and Denison's Law." *Journal of Political Economy* 82 (1974), 225–50.

[84] E. Gramlich. "Infrastructure Investment: A Review Essay." *Journal of Economic Literature* 32.3 (1994), 1176–96.

[85] B. Baltagi and N. Pinnoi. "Public Capital and State Productivity Growth." *Empirical Economics* 20 (1995), 351–59.

[86] P. Bom and J. Ligthart. "What Have We Learned from Three Decades of Research on the Productivity of Public Capital?" *Journal of Economic Surveys* 28.5 (2014), 889–916.

[87] C. Lynde and J. Richmond. "The Role of Public Capital in Production." *The Review of Economics and Statistics* 74.1 (1992), 37–44.

[88] V. Duggal, C. Saltzman, and L. Klein. "Infrastructure and Productivity: A Nonlinear Approach." *Journal of Econometrics* 92 (1999), 47–74.

[89] E. Berndt and B. Hansson. "Measuring the Contribution of Public Infrastructure Capital in Sweden." NBER Working Paper No. 3842. 1991.

[90] J. P. Cohen and C. Paul. "Public Infrastructure Investment, Interstate Spatial Spillovers, and Manufacturing Costs." *The Review of Economics and Statistics* 86.2 (2004), 551–60.

[91] P. Demetriades and T. Mamuneas. "Intertemporal Output and Employment Effects of Public Infrastructure Capital: Evidence from 12 OECD Economies." *The Economic Journal* 110 (2000), 687–712.

[92] C. Hulten, , E. Bennathan, and S. Srinivasan. "Infrastructure, Externalities, and Economic Development: A Study of Indian Manufacturing Industry." *World Bank Economic Review* 20 (2006), 291–308.

[93] V. Duggal, C. Saltzman, and L. Klein. "Infrastructure and Productivity: An Extension to Private Infrastructure and IT Productivity." *Journal of Econometrics* 140 (2007), 485–502.

[94] J. Rud. "Electricity provision and industrial development: Evidence from India." *Journal of Development Economics* 97 (2012), 352–67.

[95] W. Easterly and S. Rebelo. "Fiscal Policy and Economic Growth: An Empirical Investigation." *Journal of Monetary Economics* 32.3 (1993), 417–58.

[96] B. Egert, T. Kozluk, and D. Sutherland. "Infrastructure and Growth: Empirical Evidence." OECD Working Paper No. 685. 2009.

[97] J. Crihfield and M. Panggabean. "Is Public Infrastructure Productive? A Metropolitan Perspective Using New Capital Stock Estimates." *Regional Science and Urban Economics* 25 (1995), 607–30.

[98] Devarajan S., V. V. Swaroop, and H. Zou. "The Composition of Public Expenditure and Economic Growth." *Journal of Monetary Economics* 37 (1996), 313–44.

[99] S. Gupta, B. Clements, E. Baldacci, and C. Mulas-Granados. "Fiscal Policy, Expenditure Composition, and Growth in Low-Income Countries." *Journal of International Money and Finance* 24 (2005), 441–63.

[100] K. Seethepalli, M. Bramati, and D. Veredas. "How Relevant Is Infrastructure to Growth in East Asia." World Bank Policy Research Working Paper Series No. 4597. 2008.

[101] G. Ingram and C. Kessides. "Infrastructure for Development." *Finance and Development*. Vol. 31.3. International Monetary Fund, 1994.

[102] H. Aaron. "Discussion of Why Is Infrastructure Important?" In *Is There a Shortfall in Public Capital Investment?* Ed. by A. Munnell. Federal Reserve Bank of Boston, 1990, pp. 51–63.

[103] D. Jorgenson. "Fragile Statistical Foundations: The Macroeconomics of Public Infrastructure Investment." American Enterprise Institute Discussion Paper. 1991.

[104] C. Hulten and R. Schwab. "Is There Too Little Public Capital? Infrastructure and Economic Growth?" American Enterprise Institute Conference Paper. 1991.

[105] C. Calderon, E. MoralBenito, and L. Serven. "Is Infrastructure Capital Productive? A Dynamic Heterogeneous Approach." *Journal of Applied Econometrics* 30.2 (2015), 177–98.

[106] J. Tatom. "Public Capital and Private Sector Performance." *Review, Federal Reserve Bank of St. Louis* 73 (1991), 3–15.

[107] P. Evans and G. Karras. "Are Government Activities Productive? Evidence from a Panel of US States." *Review of Economics and Statistics* 76.1 (1994), 1–11.

[108] WorldBank. "Private Participation in Infrastructure: Half Year report." 2021.

[109] R. Gillanders. "Corruption and Infrastructure at the Country and Regional Level." *Journal of Development Studies* 50 (2014), 803–19.

[110] P. Keefer and S. Knack. "Boondoggles, Rent-Seeking and Political Checks and Balances: Public Investment under Unaccountable Governments." *Review of Economics and Statistics* 89 (2007), 566–72.

[111] C. Kenny. "Measuring Corruption in Infrastructure: Evidence from Transition and Developing Countries." *Journal of Development Studies* 45.3 (2009), 314–32.

[112] C. Kilby. "The Political Economy of Project Preparation: An Empirical Analysis of World Bank Projects." *Journal of Development Economics* 105 (2013), 211–25.

[113] L. Pritchett. "The Tyranny of Concepts: CUDIE (Cumulated, Depreciated, Investment Effort) Is Not Capital." *Journal of Economic Growth* 5.4 (2000), 361–84.

[114] L. Rubin. "Productivity and the Public Capital Stock: Another Look." Federal Reserve Board Discussion Paper No. 118. 1991.

[115] G. Olley and A. Pakes. "The Dynamics of Productivity in the Telecommunications Equipment Industry." *Econometrica* 64.6 (1996), 1263–97.

[116] A. Collard-Wexler and J. De Loecker. "Production Function Estimation and Capital Measurement Error." NBER Working Paper No. 22437. 2020.

[117] K. Sinha and S. Labi. *Transportation Decision-Making Principles of Project Evaluation and Programming*. John Wiley Sons, Inc, 2007.

[118] R. Cervero. "Linking Urban Transport and Land Use in Developing Countries." *Journal of Transport and Land Use* 6.1 (2013), 7–24.

[119] G. Michaels. "The Effect of Trade on the Demand for Skill: Evidence from the Interstate Highway System." *The Review of Economics and Statistics* 90.4 (2008), 683–701.

[120] G. Duranton and M. Turner. "The Fundamental Law of Road Congestion: Evidence from US Cities." *American Economic Review* 101.6 (2011), 2616–52.

[121] S. Datta. "The Impact of Improved Highways on Indian Firms." *Journal of Development Economics* 99 (2012), 46–57.

[122] A. Pereira and O. Roca-Sagales. "Spillover Effects of Public Capital Formation: Evidence from the Spanish Regions." *Journal of Urban Economics* 53 (2003), 238–56.

[123] M. Boarnet. "Spillovers and the Locational Effects of Public Infrastructure." *Journal of Regional Science* 38.3 (1998), 381–400.

[124] D. Donaldson and R. Hornbeck. "Railroads and American Economic Growth: A Market Access Approach." *Quarterly Journal of Economics* 131.2 (2016), 799–858.

[125] C. Bai and Y. Qian. "Infrastructure Development in China: The Cases of Electricity, Highways, and Railways." *Journal of Comparative Economics* 38 (2010), 34–51.

[126] B. Faber. "Trade Integration, Market Size, and Industrialization: Evidence from China's National Trunk Highway System Get access Arrow." *The Review of Economic Studies* 81.3 (2014), 1046–70.

[127] D. Donaldson. "Railroads of the Raj: Estimating the Impact of Transportation Infrastructure." *American Economic Review* 108.4–5 (2018), 899–934.

[128] E. Ghani, A. Goswami, and W. Kerr. "Highway to Success: The Impact of the Golden Quadrilateral Project for the Location and Performance of Indian Manufacturing." *Economic Journal* 126.591 (2016), 317–57.

[129] J. Asturias, M. Garcia-Santana, and R. Ramos. "Competition and the Welfare Gains from Transportation Infrastructure: Evidence from the Golden Quadrilateral of India." *Journal of the European Economic Association* 17.6 (2018), 1881–940.

[130] N. Baum-Snow, L. Brandt, J. Henderson, M. Turner, and Q. Zhang. "Roads, Railroads, and Decentralization of Chinese Cities." *The Review of Economics and Statistics* 99.3 (2017), 435–48.

[131] N. Baum-Snow. "Did Highways Cause Suburbanization?" *Quarterly Journal of Economics* 122.2 (2007), 775–805.

[132] N. Limao and A. Venables. "Infrastructure, Geographical Disadvantage, Transport Costs, and Trade." *The World Bank Economic Review* 15.3 (2001), 451–79.

[133] X. Diao and Y. Yanoma. "Exploring Regional Dynamics in Sub-Saharan African Agriculture." IFPRI DSGD Discussion Paper No. 2. 2003.

[134] R. Reinikka and J. Svensson. "How Inadequate Provision of Public Infrastructure and Services Affects Private Investment." The World Bank, Policy Research Working Paper Series No. 2262. 1999.

[135] K. Lumbila. "What Makes FDI Work? A Panel Analysis of the Growth Effect of FDI in Africa." Africa Region Working Paper Series No. 80, The World Bank. 2005.

[136] B. Lewis. "The Impact of Public Infrastructure on Municipal Economic Development: Empirical Results from Kenya." *Review of Urban and Regional Development Studies* 10.2 (1998), 142–56.

[137] S. Boopen. "Transport Infrastructure and Economic Growth: Evidence from Africa Using Dynamic Panel Estimates." *The Empirical Economic Letters* 5.1 (2006), 37–52.

[138] O. Kodongo and K. Ojah. "Does Infrastructure Really Explain Economic Growth in Sub-Saharan Africa?" *Review of Development Finance* 6.2 (2016), 105–25.

[139] J. Mostert and J. Van Heerden. "A Computable General Equilibrium Analysis of the Expenditure on Infrastructure in the Limpopo Economy in South Africa." *International Advances in Economic Research* 21.2 (2015), 227–36.

[140] M. Ayogu. "Before Prebendalism: A Positive Analysis of Core Infrastructure Investment in a Developing Fiscal Federalism." *African Development Review* 11.2 (1999), 169–98.

[141] C. Kularatne. "Social and Economic Infrastructure Impacts on Economic Growth in South Africa." www.tips.org.za/files/forum/2006/papers/SocialandEconomicInfrastructure.pdf. 2005.

[142] T. Dinkelman. "The Effects of Rural Electrification on Employment: New Evidence from South Africa." *American Economic Review* 101.7 (2011), 3078–108.

[143] W. Mitchell. "The Backward Art of Spending Money." *American Economic Review* 2.2 (1912), 269–81.

[144] S. Kuznets. "National Income." *National Bureau of Economic Research, Research Bulletin* 49 (1934), 1929–32.

[145] G. Becker. "A Theory of the Allocation of Time." *Economic Journal* 75.299 (1965), 493–517.

[146] G. Ghez and G. Becker. "The Allocation of Time and Goods over the Life Cycle." New York: National Bureau of Economic Research. 1975.

[147] G. Becker. "Human Capital and the Personal Distribution of Income: An Analytical Approach." In *Human Capital: A Theoretical and Empirical Analysis, with Special Reference to Education*. 2nd ed. National Bureau of Economic Research, 1975.

[148] G. Becker. "Human Capital: A Theoretical and Empirical Analysis, With Special Reference to Education." National Bureau of Economic Research,. 1964.

[149] G. Becker. "Irrational Behavior and Economic Theory." *Journal of Political Economy* 70.1 (1962), 1–13.

[150] J. Mincer. "Investment in Human Capital and Personal Income Distribution." *Journal of Political Economy* 66.4 (1958), 281–302.

[151] J. Mincer. "On-the-Job Training: Costs, Returns, and Some Implications." *Journal of Political Economy* 706.5 (1962), 50–79.

[152] J. Mincer. *Schooling, Experience and Earnings*. Columbia University Press, 1974.

[153] Y. Ben-Porath. "The Production of Human Capital and the Life Cycle of Earnings." *Journal of Political Economy* 75.4 (1967), 352–65.

[154] A. Leibowitz. "Home Investments in Children." *Journal of Political Economy* 82.2 (1974), S111–S31.

[155] F. Cunha and J. Heckman. "The Technology of Skill Formation." *American Economic Review* 97.2 (2007), 31–47.

[156] G. Becker and H. Lewis. "On the Interaction between the Quantity and Quality of Children." *Journal of Political Economy* 81.2 (1973), S279–S88.

[157] F. Juster and F. Stafford. *Time, Goods, and Well-Being*. Institute for Social Research, University of Michigan, 1985.

[158] M. Aguiar and E. Hurst. "Measuring Trends in Leisure: The Allocation of Time over Five Decades." *Quarterly Journal of Economics* 122.3 (2007), 969–1006.

[159] R. Gronau. *The Value of Time in Passenger Transportation: The Demand for Air Travel*. Columbia University Press, 1970.

[160] J. Smits and R. Steendijk. "The International Wealth Index (IWI)." *Social Indicators Research* 122.1 (2015), 65–85.

[161] F. Paumgarten and C. Shackleton. "The Role of Non-timber Forest Products in Household Coping Strategies In South Africa: The Influence of Household Wealth and Gender." *Population and Environment* 33 (2011), 1263–97.

[162] H. Swaminathan, R. Lahoti, and J. Suchitra. "Gender Asset and Wealth Gaps: Evidence from Karnataka." *Economic and Political Weekly* 47.35 (2012), 59–67.

[163] S. Claessens. "Access to Financial Services: A Review of the Issues and Public Policy Objectives." *The World Bank Research Observer* 21.2 (2006), 207–40.

[164] L. Stein and C. Yannelis. "Financial Inclusion, Human Capital, and Wealth Accumulation: Evidence from the Freedmans Savings Bank." *The Review of Financial Studies* 33.11 (2020), 5333–77.

[165] DHS. "Standard Recode Manual for DHS 7." USAID. 2018.

[166] C. Freire, K. Macmanus, M. Pesaresi, E. Doxsey-Whitfield and J. Mills. "Development of New Open and Free Multi-Temporal Global Population Grids at 250 m Resolution. Geospatial Data in a Changing World." Association of Geographic Information Laboratories in Europe (AGILE). 2016.

[167] C. Linard and A. Tatem. "Large-Scale Spatial Population Databases in Infectious Disease Research." *International Journal of Health Geographics* 11.1 (2012), 1–13.

[168] D. Weiss, A. Nelson, H. S. Gibson et al. "A Global Map of Travel Time to Cities to Assess Inequalities in Accessibility in 2015." *Nature* 553 (2018), 333–336.

[169] GTOP. "Earth Resources Observation and Science Center." Global 30 Arc-Second Elevation (GTOPO30). 1996.

[170] S. Demurger. "Infrastructure Development and Economic Growth: An Explanation for Regional Disparities in China?" *Journal of Comparative Economics* 29.1 (2001), 95–117.

[171] S. Fan and X. Zhang. "Infrastructure and Regional Economic Development in Rural China." *China Economic Review* 15.2 (2004), 203–14.

[172] H. Esfahani and M. Ramirez. "Institutions, Infrastructure and Economic Growth." *Journal of Development Economics* 70.2 (2003), 443–77.

[173] O. Cadot, L. Roller, and A. Stephan. "Contribution to Productivity or Pork Barrel? The Two Faces of Infrastructure Investment." *Journal of Public Economics* 90 (2006), 1133–53.

[174] L. Hansen. "Large Sample Properties of Generalized Method of Moments Estimators." *Econometrica* 50.3 (1982), 1029–54.

[175] D. Aschauer. "Is Public Expenditure Productive?" *Journal of Monetary Economics* 23.2 (1989), 177–200.

[176] J. Scholz and A. Seshadri. "Children and Household Wealth." Michigan Retirement Research Center Research Paper No. WP 2007–158. 2007.

[177] B. Shaukat, S. Javed, and W. Imran. "Wealth Index as Substitute to Income and Consumption: Assessment of Household Poverty Determinants Using Demographic and Health Survey Data." *Journal of Poverty* 24.1 (2020), 24–44.

[178] Y. Wang, Y. Li, Y. Huang, C. Yi, and J. Ren. "Housing Wealth Inequality in China: An Urban–Rural Comparison." *Cities* 96 (2020).

[179] WorldBank. *The Living Standard Measurement Study.* www.worldbank.org/en/programs/lsms.

[180] G. Clarke, L. Xu, and H. Zou. "Finance and Income Inequality: Test of Alternative Theories." *Annals of Economics and Finance* 14.2 (2013), 493–510.

[181] A. Demirguc-Kunt and R. Levine. *Financial Structure and Economic Growth: A Cross-Country Comparison of Banks, Markets, and Development.* MIT Press, 2004.

[182] T. Beck, R. Levine, and N. Loayza. "Finance and the Sources of Growth." *Journal of Financial Economics* 58.1–2 (2000), 261–300.

[183] A. Demirguc-Kunt and V. Maksimovic. "Law, Finance, and Firm Growth." *Journal of Finance* 53.6 (1998), 2107–37.

[184] R. Rajan and L. Zingales. "Financial Development and Growth." *American Economic Review* 88.3 (1998), 559–86.

[185] E. Glaeser, M. Kahn, and J. Rappaport. "Why Do the Poor Live in Cities? The Role of Public Transportation." *Journal of Urban Economics* 63.1 (2008), 1–24.

[186] K. Emmanuel. "Government Sets Up Committee to Disburse Cash to June 3 Disaster Victims." www.pulse.com.gh/news/local/govt-sets-up-committee-to-disburse-cash-to-june-3-disaster-victims/t95myj6. 2019.

[187] R. Davies. "Ghana – Major Roads, Bridges and Over 100 Homes Destroyed in Upper West Region Floods." Floodlist [Online]. https://floodlist.com/africa/ghana-major-roads-bridges-and-over-100-homes-destroyed-in-upper-west-region-floods. 2021.

[188] T. W. Anderson. "Estimating Linear Restrictions on Regression Coefficients for Multivariate Normal Distributions." *Annals of Mathematical Statistics* 22 (1951), 327–51.

[189] J. G. Cragg and S. G. Donald. "Testing Identifiability and Specification in Instrumental Variables Models." *Econometric Theory* 9 (1993), 222–40.

[190] E. Sanderson and F. Windmeijer. "A Weak Instrument F-test in Linear IV Models with Multiple Endogenous Variables." *Journal of Econometrics* 190.2 (2016), 212–21.

[191] T. W. Anderson and H. Rubin. "Estimation of the Parameters of a Single Equation in a Complete System of Stochastic Equations." *Annals of Mathematical Statistics* 20 (1949), 46–63.

[192] J.H. Stock and J.H. Wright. "GMM with Weak Identification." *Econometrica* 68.5 (2000), 1055–96.

[193] W. Crain and L. Oakley. "The Politics of Infrastructure." *Journal of Law and Economics* 38 (1995), 1–17.

[194] W. Henisz. "The Institutional Environment for Infrastructure Investment." *Industrial and Corporate Change* 11 (2002), 355–89.

[195] C. Cantarelli, B. Flybjerg, E. Molin, and B. van Wee. "Cost Overruns in Large-Scale Transportation Infrastructure Projects: Explanations and Their Theoretical Embeddedness." *European Journal of Transport and Infrastructure Research* 10 (2010), 5–18.

[196] A. Rodriguez-Pose. "Economic Convergence and Regional Development Strategies in Spain: The Case of Galicia and Navarre." *European Investment Bank* 5 (2000), 89–115.

[197] GADM. https://gadm.org/downloadcountry.html. GADM Data. 2022.

Acknowledgments

This Element is based on the authors' research on the impacts of infrastructure in the case of Ghana. We are grateful for constructive comments from Godwin Okafor, Zheng Wang, Nhan Le, Georgios Kitsoleris, and participants in the Vietnam Symposium on International Business. We thank Theu Dinh for providing excellent editorial support. We also thank the Institute for Applied Economics and Social Value (IAESV) and the Association of Vietnamese Scientists and Experts (AVSE) for their continuing support throughout this research.

Cambridge Elements ☰

Economics of Emerging Markets

Bruno S. Sergi
Harvard University

Editor Bruno S. Sergi is an instructor at Harvard University, an associate of the Harvard University Davis Center for Russian and Eurasian Studies and Harvard Ukrainian Research Institute. He is Academic Series Editor of the Cambridge *Elements in the Economics of Emerging Markets* (Cambridge University Press), a co-editor of the *Lab for Entrepreneurship and Development* book series, and associate editor of *The American Economist*. Concurrently, he teaches International Economics at the University of Messina, is Scientific Director of the Lab for Entrepreneurship and Development (LEAD), and a co-founder and Scientific Director of the International Center for Emerging Markets Research at RUDN University in Moscow. He has published over 150 articles in professional journals and twenty-one books as author, co-author, editor, and co-editor.

About the Series

The aim of this Elements series is to deliver state-of-the-art, comprehensive coverage of the knowledge developed to date, including the dynamics and prospects of these economies, focusing on emerging markets' economics, finance, banking, technology advances, trade, demographic challenges, and their economic relations with the rest of the world, as well as the causal factors and limits of economic policy in these markets.

Cambridge Elements ⁼

Economics of Emerging Markets

A full series listing is available at: www.cambridge.org/EEM

Printed in the United States
by Baker & Taylor Publisher Services